The Type 2 Diabetes Cookbook for Newly Diagnosed 2024

Eating Well with Type 2 Diabetes; Your Guide to Irresistible and Affordable Recipes for Managing Type 2 Diabetes with a Versatile 30-Day Meal Plan

Thank you so much for choosing to purchase our book! We truly appreciate your support. Positive reviews and ratings from fantastic readers like you mean a great deal to us. Your feedback not only encourages us but also fuels our passion for creating books that resonate with our readers. We're eager to hear your thoughts and can't wait to know what you think.

Once again, thank you for being a valued reader.

Best regards,
Juliana C. Huggins

Table Of Content

Introduction...6

    Welcome to Eating Well with Type 2 Diabetes...6

    Navigating Type 2 Diabetes... 10

    The Power of Food and Meal Planning: Your Roadmap to Health and Well-being.... 12

    Essential Cooking Tips for Diabetes Management: Mastering Your Kitchen for Health 15

Breakfast (Quick & Easy for Busy Mornings):.. 18

    Sweet & Savory Options:..18

        Yogurt Parfait with Berries & Granola:.................................... 18

        Scrambled Eggs with Spinach & Toast:.....................................18

        Overnight Oats with Chia Seeds & Fruit:................................... 19

        Banana Smoothie with Spinach & Nut Butter:..............................20

        Cottage Cheese Toast with Sliced Tomatoes & Herbs:.................... 21

        Whole-Wheat English Muffins with Avocado & Poached Egg:............21

        Chia Seed Pudding with Almond Milk & Fruit:.............................22

        Breakfast Burrito with Scrambled Eggs & Veggies:....................... 23

        Smoothie Bowl with Greek Yogurt, Granola & Nuts:...................... 24

        Baked Sweet Potato Toast with Toasted Nuts & Honey:....................24

    Quick & Convenient:..25

        Hard-boiled Eggs with Whole-Wheat Toast & Avocado:..................25

        Whole-wheat Waffles with Greek Yogurt & Berries:...................... 26

        Nut Butter & Banana Sandwich on Whole-Wheat Bread:................. 27

        Protein Bar with Fruit & Greek Yogurt....................................... 27

        Trail Mix with Yogurt & Honey: A Nourishing Grab-and-Go Breakfast.............28

        Edamame Pods with Sea Salt & Sriracha:................................... 29

        Cottage Cheese with Sliced Cucumbers & Herbs:......................... 30

        Avocado Toast with Everything Bagel Seasoning:......................... 30

        Greek Yogurt with Chia Seeds & Honey:................................... 31

        Fruit Salad with Coconut Yogurt & Granola:............................... 32

Lunch (Delicious & Nutritious Midday Meals)..33

    Salads with Flair:...33

        Mediterranean Chickpea Salad:...33

        Southwest Fiesta Salad:..33

        Quinoa & Grilled Chicken Salad:...34

        Asian Noodle Salad with Peanut Dressing:................................35

Soups for Every Season:...37

   Creamy Tomato Bisque:.. 37

   Spicy Lentil Stew:..38

   Chilled Cucumber Gazpacho:...39

   Black Bean Soup with Avocado Salsa.......................................39

Sandwiches Reinvented:..41

   Grilled Portobello with Goat Cheese:.......................................41

   Turkey & Cranberry Wraps:... 41

   Vegetarian Pita Pockets:..42

   Tuna Salad Lettuce Wraps:.. 43

One-Pan Wonders:..45

   Sheet Pan Salmon with Veggies:.. 45

   Lemon Chicken with Asparagus:...45

   Spicy Shrimp Scampi with Linguine...46

Slow Cooker Solutions..48

   Beef Chili with Black Beans:..48

   Moroccan Chicken Tagine:...49

   Creamy White Bean Stew (Slow Cooker or Stovetop):.............. 49

Wraps & Bowls.. 52

   Hummus Veggie Wraps:...52

   Buddha Bowl with Quinoa & Tahini Dressing:..........................52

   Chicken Caesar Salad Wraps:...53

Light & Refreshing...55

   Caprese Salad with Grilled Halloumi:.......................................55

   Mediterranean Couscous Salad:..55

Warm & Comforting:.. 57

   Chicken Pot Pie Soup:... 57

   Lentil Shepherd's Pie:..58

Global Flavors at Home:... 60

   Thai Shrimp Curry:..60

   Italian Meatballs with Zucchini Noodles:..................................61

   Korean Bibimbap Bowls:..62

   Falafel Pita Pockets:..63

Family-Friendly & Flavorful Dinner Ideas for Every Night:................. 65

Quick & Easy Weeknight Delights:..65

   One-Pan Chicken Fajitas:...65

Creamy Tomato Pasta with Spinach:..66

Salmon with Lemon & Broccoli:...66

Turkey Burgers with Sweet Potato Fries:...67

Pizza Night Done Right: Two Delicious and Customizable Options...................68

Slow Cooker Solutions for Busy Days:...71

Honey Garlic Chicken & Veggies:..71

Pulled Pork Tacos:..71

Lentil & Vegetable Soup:..73

Beef Chili:..73

Chicken Curry with Coconut Milk:..75

Global Flavors at Home:...76

Stir-Fried Chicken & Veggies:...76

Taco Tuesday with a Twist: Three Flavorful Variations to Spice Up Your Night!.77

Pasta Primavera with Spring Veggies: A Burst of Freshness for Your Palette.......79

Mediterranean Salmon with Lemon & Herbs:...80

Sheet Pan Fajita Bowls:...81

Weekend Feasts & Potlucks:...83

Lasagna Roll-Ups:...83

Chicken Pot Pie:...84

Beef & Broccoli Stir-Fry:...85

Sheet Pan Roasted Chicken & Vegetables:..86

One-Pot Pasta Primavera:...87

Plant-Based Powerhouses:..89

Black Bean Burgers: Two Delicious and Customizable Versions.......................89

Lentil Shepherd's Pie:...90

Tofu Scramble with Veggies:...91

Pasta Primavera with Pesto:..92

Mushroom & Lentil Bolognese:...93

Satisfying & Blood Sugar-Friendly Snacks & Sides:...95

Fresh & Crunchy:..95

Carrot sticks with hummus or avocado dip:...95

Apple slices with almond butter:..96

Celery sticks with peanut butter and raisins:..96

Bell pepper slices with cottage cheese:...97

Edamame pods with sea salt:..98

Dips & Spreads:..100

Roasted vegetable crudités with Greek yogurt dip:..100

Homemade guacamole with whole-wheat crackers:...101

Black bean salsa with whole-wheat chips:..101

Roasted chickpeas with spices:..102

Hard-boiled eggs with whole-wheat bread:...103

Fruits & Yogurt:...105

Berry parfait with Greek yogurt and granola:...105

Sliced pears with ricotta cheese and honey:...106

Frozen yogurt bark with berries and nuts:..106

Fruit salad with chia seeds and coconut flakes:..107

Baked apples with cinnamon and nuts:..108

Veggie-Based Bowls:...110

Mixed green salad with grilled chicken or tofu and vinaigrette:...........................110

Quinoa salad with roasted vegetables and balsamic glaze:..................................111

Lentil soup with whole-wheat bread:...112

Spiralized zucchini noodles with tomato sauce and meatballs:.............................113

Roasted Brussels sprouts with balsamic glaze and pecans:..................................114

Extras:...116

Air-popped popcorn with spices:..116

Dark chocolate with nuts and dried fruit:...116

Homemade trail mix with nuts, seeds, and dried fruit: Your Customizable & Nutritious Powerhouse Snack...118

Roasted Sweet Potato Wedges with Herbs: A Delicious & Healthy Side Dish....119

Yogurt bark with sliced vegetables and herbs:..119

Bonus Resources:...121

3O-Day Meal Plan For Type 2 Diabetes Management...121

Grocery Shopping Guide for Diabetics..126

Festive Holiday Recipes for Diverse Dietary Needs:...129

Vegan & Delicious:...129

Low-Carb & Satisfying:...134

Gluten-Free Goodies:..139

For Everyone Enjoying:..144

Additional Recipes for Inspiration:..149

Introduction

Welcome to Eating Well with Type 2 Diabetes

A Delicious, Nutritious, and Empowered Journey to Health

Congratulations on taking the first step towards managing your Type 2 diabetes! You've probably heard conflicting information about food, what to eat, and what to avoid. But the truth is, managing your diabetes through a diet isn't about deprivation or fad diets. It's about discovering a vibrant new relationship with food, one that prioritizes deliciousness, health, and empowerment.

This guide is your companion on this exciting journey. We'll explore the basics of Type 2 diabetes, debunk common myths, and equip you with the tools and knowledge to:
- Fuel your body with nutritious, satisfying meals.
- Cook up amazing dishes that taste incredible and support your blood sugar goals.
- Become a confident chef in your own kitchen.
- Embrace food as a powerful tool for your health and well-being.

So, let's gets started;

Understanding Type 2 Diabetes:

Imagine your body as a well-oiled machine. Insulin, a hormone produced by your pancreas, acts like a key that unlocks your cells, allowing the sugar (glucose) from your food to enter and be used for energy. In Type 2 diabetes, this key either doesn't work properly (insulin resistance) or your body doesn't produce enough insulin. This leads to elevated blood sugar levels, which can harm your health over time.

But here's the good news: You have the power to manage your blood sugar through healthy eating, regular physical activity, and, if needed, medication. Food is your fuel, and choosing the right foods can make a significant difference in how you feel and how your body functions.

Debunking the Myths:

- Myth: You can't eat sugar or any carbohydrates if you have diabetes.
- Fact: You can enjoy all types of food in moderation while focusing on whole, unprocessed options. Prioritize fruits, vegetables, whole grains, lean protein, and healthy fats.
- Myth: You have to eat bland, boring food.

- Fact: Eating well with diabetes means exploring a world of flavorful, exciting recipes. You can still enjoy your favorite dishes with modifications and healthier ingredients.
- Myth: Managing diabetes is too complicated.
- Fact: With the right guidance and support, you can easily develop healthy eating habits that become second nature.

Your Toolkit for Success:

Now, let's equip you with the tools you need to succeed:

- Plate Power: This visual guide helps you portion your meals for balanced blood sugar control. Fill half your plate with non-starchy vegetables, a quarter with lean protein, and a quarter with whole grains or starchy vegetables.
- Glycemic Index (GI): This helps you understand how quickly certain foods raise your blood sugar. Opt for low-GI foods for sustained energy and blood sugar control.
- Reading Food Labels: Become familiar with serving sizes, carbohydrates, and added sugars to make informed choices.
- Meal Planning: Planning your meals helps you stay on track and avoid unhealthy temptations.

Embrace the Kitchen:

Cooking doesn't have to be daunting! Start with simple, delicious recipes that use fresh, whole ingredients. Experiment with different flavors and spices to find what you love. Remember, the more you enjoy the food you eat, the more likely you are to stick with it.

Here are some recipe ideas to get you started:

- Breakfast: Blueberry Greek yogurt with chia seeds and almonds, scrambled eggs with spinach and whole-wheat toast, overnight oats with berries and nuts.
- Lunch: Quinoa salad with grilled chicken and avocado, lentil soup with whole-wheat bread, tuna salad lettuce wraps.
- Dinner: Salmon with roasted vegetables, turkey chili with kidney beans and brown rice, vegetarian stir-fry with tofu and brown rice.
- Snacks: Greek yogurt with fruit and granola, apple slices with almond butter, hummus with carrot sticks, air-popped popcorn.

Remember:
- Small changes can make a big difference. Start by incorporating one or two new healthy habits into your routine each week.

- Don't be afraid to experiment. Find what works best for you and your body.
- Celebrate your successes, big and small. Every healthy choice is a step towards a healthier you.
- Seek support. Talk to your doctor, a registered dietitian, or join a diabetes support group for guidance and encouragement.

Eating well with Type 2 diabetes is not a sentence but an opportunity. It's a chance to discover a new relationship with food—one that empowers you, fuels your body, and brings joy to your life.

Remember, you are not alone on this journey. With the right support, information, and delicious recipes, you can unlock a vibrant, healthy life filled with the joy of food! This comprehensive guide is your companion on this empowering journey, offering tools and knowledge to:

- Navigate the basics of Type 2 diabetes: Understand the role of insulin, how blood sugar works, and the potential complications of uncontrolled diabetes.
- Develop a personalized meal plan
- Transform your kitchen into a haven of health: Discover essential cooking tips, pantry staples, and healthy substitutions to create delicious and diabetes-friendly recipes.

Remember, managing Type 2 diabetes is not a solitary battle. You have a multitude of resources and allies at your disposal:

- Your doctor: Your primary care physician or endocrinologist plays a crucial role in monitoring your blood sugar levels, adjusting medication if needed, and providing personalized guidance.
- Registered dietitian: A registered dietitian can translate medical information into practical dietary advice, create a personalized meal plan, and address your specific nutritional needs.
- Diabetes educator: Gain valuable insights into self-monitoring, medication management, and lifestyle modifications from a dedicated diabetes educator.
- Support groups: Connecting with others facing similar challenges offers emotional support, practical tips, and a sense of belonging.

Throughout this journey, let joy be your guiding light. Experiment with new recipes, discover the pleasure of healthy cooking, and celebrate your successes, big and small. Each nutritious meal and each step towards a healthier lifestyle is a victory worth savoring.

This guide is just the beginning. With the right tools, information, and support, you can transform your relationship with food, empower your body, and unlock a lifetime of vibrant health and happiness. Take a deep breath, embrace the opportunities that lie ahead, and step into the kitchen with confidence, knowing that you are not alone on this journey.

Bon appétit!

Navigating Type 2 Diabetes

Finding out you have Type 2 diabetes can be a lot to take in. It might make you feel confused and scared. You may have many questions like, "What does this mean for my life?" or "How do I handle this?" This guide is here to help you through this tough time.

Living with Type 2 Diabetes:

Living with Type 2 diabetes doesn't have to mean drastic life changes. It's about making sustainable, smart adjustments to your existing lifestyle. Here are some areas to focus on:

- Diet: This is where food becomes your medicine. Prioritizing whole, unprocessed foods like fruits, vegetables, whole grains, and lean protein will provide your body with the nutrients it needs while balancing your blood sugar. Learn about smart carbohydrate choices, glycemic index, and portion control. Remember, it's not about deprivation but about making informed choices that taste good and nourish your body.
- Exercise: Regular physical activity helps your body utilize insulin more effectively, lowering blood sugar levels. Find activities you enjoy, whether it's brisk walking, swimming, dancing, or anything that gets your heart pumping. Start gradually and build your activity level over time.
- Stress Management: Chronic stress can negatively impact your blood sugar levels. Find healthy ways to manage stress, like yoga, meditation, spending time in nature, or connecting with loved ones. Prioritize activities that bring you joy and relaxation.
- Sleep: Good sleep is essential for overall health, including blood sugar control. Aim for 7-8 hours of quality sleep each night. Establish a regular sleep schedule and create a relaxing bedtime routine.

Technology and Tools:

- Blood Glucose Monitoring: Utilizing a blood glucose meter and regularly monitoring your levels equips you with crucial data to understand how your body reacts to different foods and activities. Discuss with your doctor how often and when to monitor your blood sugar.
- Continuous Glucose Monitoring (CGM): This advanced technology provides real-time blood sugar readings through a sensor inserted under the skin. While not for everyone, CGM can offer valuable insights for some individuals aiming for tight blood sugar control.
- Diabetes Apps: Numerous apps can enhance your diabetes management, ranging from food logging and carbohydrate counting to exercise tracking and medication reminders. Explore and find apps that cater to your specific needs and preferences.

Beyond Diet and Exercise:

- Mental Health and Diabetes: The emotional rollercoaster of a new diagnosis can significantly impact your mental well-being. Prioritize your mental health by practicing stress management techniques, seeking professional help if needed, and connecting with loved ones for support.
- Financial Considerations: Managing diabetes can involve additional expenses for medication, equipment, and healthy food choices. Talk to your healthcare team about available resources and financial assistance programs that can help navigate these costs.
- Cultural Influences and Food Choices: Cultural food traditions and beliefs can greatly influence dietary patterns. Acknowledge and respect your cultural background while adapting your eating habits to incorporate healthy choices within your cultural framework.

Looking Ahead:

- Research and Advancements: The field of diabetes research is constantly evolving, offering new treatment options and technologies. Stay informed about promising advancements and discuss them with your doctor to determine how they might fit into your management plan.
- Advocacy and Support: Be an advocate for yourself and others living with diabetes. Join advocacy groups, raise awareness, and participate in research studies to contribute to improving care and management for future generations.
- Living a Fulfilling Life: Type 2 diabetes may be a lifelong companion, but it doesn't define you. Remember to find joy in life, pursue your passions, and embrace the many possibilities that lie ahead.

This is just a glimpse into the vast world of information and resources available to empower your journey with Type 2 diabetes. Remember, knowledge is power, and the more you learn about your condition, the more confident and empowered you will become in managing it and living a healthy, fulfilling life.

Let this be the beginning of your empowering journey, not the end!

The Power of Food and Meal Planning: Your Roadmap to Health and Well-being

Food isn't just fuel; it's a powerful tool for shaping our health, our energy levels, and even our happiness. For those living with Type 2 diabetes, this power becomes even more pronounced. Food choices and meal planning can revolutionize your relationship with your body, empower you to manage your condition, and unlock a vibrant, healthy life.

This guide dives deep into the synergy between food and meal planning as it pertains to Type 2 diabetes. We'll explore:

- Why food matters: Understanding the intricate connection between your food choices and blood sugar levels.
- The magic of meal planning: Discover how planning your meals empowers you to make informed choices, reduce stress, and stay on track.
- Building a diabetes-friendly plate: Learn simple yet effective principles for constructing balanced and satisfying meals.
- Beyond the recipe: Uncover tips and tricks for navigating temptation, staying motivated, and making meal planning a joyful experience.

Food: Your Secret Weapon:

Think of food as a symphony of colors, textures, and nutrients that orchestrate your internal orchestra. Carbohydrates provide the melody, fueling your cells. Protein serves as the rhythm, maintaining muscle mass and satiety. Healthy fats add the bassline, supporting cellular functions and keeping you feeling full. And vitamins, minerals, and antioxidants sprinkle in the magic, protecting your body from harm.

In Type 2 diabetes, the conductor, insulin, faces some challenges. Carbohydrates, the melody, can sometimes cause blood sugar to spike, throwing the orchestra into disarray. But don't silence the music! Instead, learn to play a harmonious tune by:

- Prioritizing whole, unprocessed foods: Think fruits, vegetables, whole grains, lean protein, and healthy fats. They offer a symphony of nutrients in their natural orchestration, promoting sustained energy and blood sugar control.
- Mindful carbohydrate choices: Not all carbs are created equal. Choose low-glycemic index (GI) options like non-starchy vegetables, whole grains, and legumes. They release sugar slowly, preventing blood sugar spikes and keeping the music smooth.
- Portion control: Every instrument needs space to shine, but too much of one can disrupt the harmony. Understand your recommended carbohydrate intake and portion your meals accordingly, ensuring each element plays its role without overpowering the others.

Meal Planning:

Think of meal planning as your personal conductor's baton, orchestrating your week's food choices with intention and ease. It's not about strict rules, but about creating a framework for success, eliminating the daily scramble of "what's for dinner?" and empowering you to make informed choices:

- Plan with purpose: Identify your goals, whether it's weight management, blood sugar control, or simply eating more vegetables. Tailor your meal plan to align with these goals, choosing recipes that support them.
- Batch cooking is your friend: Cook bigger portions of healthy meals on weekends and store them for the week. This eliminates the daily pressure of cooking and ensures you have delicious, diabetes-friendly options readily available.
- Grocery shopping with focus: Make a list based on your meal plan and stick to it! Avoid impulse purchases that might disrupt your carefully orchestrated symphony.
- Variety is key: Keep your orchestra vibrant by exploring different recipes and cuisines. You can enjoy delicious meals while ensuring you get the diverse nutrients your body needs.

Building a Balanced Plate:

Think of your plate as your canvas and each meal as a beautiful masterpiece. Here's how to compose a diabetes-friendly masterpiece:

- Half the plate: Non-starchy vegetables: Broccoli, spinach, peppers, and mushrooms are your colorful chorus, bursting with fiber and vitamins that regulate blood sugar and keep you feeling full.
- Quarter of the plate: Lean protein: Chicken, fish, beans, and tofu are the sturdy pillars of your meal, providing sustained energy and building muscle mass.
- Quarter of the plate: Whole grains or starchy vegetables: Brown rice, quinoa, sweet potatoes, and corn are the melodic backdrop, offering complex carbohydrates for sustained energy without compromising blood sugar control.
- Healthy fats for the finishing touch: A drizzle of olive oil, avocado slices, or a sprinkle of nuts add the richness and satiety, without overshadowing the main melody.

Beyond the Recipe:

- Meal planning and healthy eating are journeys, not destinations. Here are some tips to keep you motivated and make the process enjoyable:
- Experiment and have fun: Try new recipes, explore different cuisines, and involve your family in the kitchen. Food should be a source of pleasure, not just fuel.
- Don't be afraid to slip up: We all have moments of indulgence. Forgive yourself, get back on track, and remember that progress, not perfection, is the key.
- Celebrate your successes: Acknowledge your achievements, no matter how small. Did you try a new vegetable? Stick to your meal plan for a week? Celebrate these milestones and keep the momentum going.
- Find your inspiration: Follow diabetes-friendly blogs, watch cooking shows, or join online communities for support and inspiration. Surrounding yourself with positive influences can keep you motivated.
- Remember, you're not alone: Many people are living with Type 2 diabetes and navigating similar challenges. Connect with others, share your experiences, and learn from each other. Your journey is unique, but you don't have to walk it alone.

The Power of Food and Meal Planning:

The journey of managing Type 2 diabetes with the power of food and meal planning isn't about deprivation or punishment. It's about discovery, empowerment, and joy. It's about learning to listen to your body, nourishing it with vibrant, delicious food, and celebrating the amazing things your body can do.

It's about taking control, not just of your blood sugar, but of your health and well-being. It's about reclaiming your kitchen, not as a battlefield, but as a stage where you create the nourishing symphony of your life.

So, pick up your plate, conduct your fork, and embark on this journey of delicious discovery. Embrace the power of food and meal planning, and find the melody that leads you to a healthier, happier, and more empowered you.

Remember, the potential for a thriving life with Type 2 diabetes lies within every bite. Take a chance, listen to your body, and let the symphony of your health begin!

Essential Cooking Tips for Diabetes Management: Mastering Your Kitchen for Health

Living with Type 2 diabetes doesn't mean sacrificing flavor or creativity in the kitchen. In fact, embracing the role of food as medicine opens up a world of possibilities for delicious and satisfying meals that support your blood sugar control and overall well-being. This guide dives deep into essential cooking tips to empower you to transform your kitchen into a hub of health and culinary adventure.

Shifting your Mindset:

Before we grab our aprons, let's shift our perspectives. It's not about restrictive diets or bland food, but about smart substitutions and mindful cooking. Embrace this as an opportunity to explore new ingredients, discover healthy alternatives, and rediscover the joy of cooking with intention. Remember, small changes add up to big results in both your health and your culinary repertoire.

Building a Diabetes-Friendly Kitchen:

Let's set you up for success with some pantry and equipment essentials:

- Pantry Staples: Stock up on whole grains like brown rice, quinoa, and oats; low-glycemic fruits like berries and apples; non-starchy vegetables like broccoli, spinach, and bell peppers; lean protein sources like chicken, fish, and beans; and healthy fats like olive oil, avocado, and nuts.
- Essential Spices: Herbs and spices add flavor without added sugar or sodium. Experiment with cinnamon, cumin, turmeric, and chili flakes to elevate your dishes.
- Kitchen Tools: Invest in a good blender for whipping up smoothies and salad dressings, a steamer for healthy vegetable preparations, and measuring cups to ensure portion control.

Mastering the Magic of Substitutions:

Substituting some key ingredients can go a long way in making your favorite recipes diabetes-friendly:

- Swap white flour for whole-wheat flour or nut flours like almond or oat flour for a fiber boost and lower glycemic index.
- Replace sugary sweeteners with natural options like stevia, monk fruit extract, or even pureed dates for a touch of sweetness.

- Choose lean protein sources over fatty cuts and incorporate plant-based proteins like lentils and beans for added variety.
- Opt for healthy fats like olive oil, avocado, and nuts instead of saturated and trans fats found in butter and processed foods.

Cooking Techniques for Optimal Health:

Embrace these methods to preserve nutrients and create delicious, healthy meals:

- Grilling, baking, and roasting preserve the natural flavors of food while minimizing unhealthy fats.
- Steaming vegetables retains their vibrant color, texture, and essential nutrients.
- Minimize added fats with cooking sprays or by poaching proteins and using broth-based sauces.
- Experiment with spices and herbs for flavor without relying on unhealthy condiments.

Portion Control: Your Plate's Compass:

Understanding and practicing portion control is key to managing blood sugar levels:

- Fill half your plate with non-starchy vegetables for essential vitamins, minerals, and fiber.
- Dedicate a quarter of your plate to lean protein for sustained energy and muscle maintenance.
- Choose whole grains or starchy vegetables for the remaining quarter for complex carbohydrates, but remember your recommended carbohydrate intake and adjust portions accordingly.
- Don't forget healthy fats! Include a small serving of avocado, nuts, or olive oil for satiety and nutrient absorption.

Beyond the Basics: Tips for Flavor and Fun:

Make healthy cooking exciting:

- Get creative with herbs and spices: Experiment with different combinations to discover new flavor profiles.
- Embrace seasonal ingredients: Fresh, local produce adds vibrancy and flavor to your meals.
- Involve your family and friends: Make cooking a social activity and get them involved in meal planning and preparation.

- Celebrate your successes: Don't be afraid to experiment and have fun! Every healthy meal is a step towards a healthier you.

Remember, managing Type 2 diabetes through cooking is a continuous journey of learning and exploration. Embrace the process, celebrate your successes, and don't be afraid to experiment! You'll be surprised at the delicious and satisfying meals you can create while supporting your health. Your kitchen is your health haven, so get creative, have fun, and empower yourself to cook up a healthier and happier you.

This is just the beginning of your culinary adventure!

Breakfast (Quick & Easy for Busy Mornings):

Sweet & Savory Options:

Yogurt Parfait with Berries & Granola:

Ingredients (for 1 serving):
- 1/2 cup plain Greek yogurt (2% fat recommended)
- 1/4 cup fresh berries (mix and match your favorites!)
- 1/4 cup granola (choose a low-sugar option for better blood sugar control)
- 1/4 teaspoon honey (optional, adjust sweetness to your preference)
- Pinch of cinnamon (optional)

Instructions:

- In a small glass or parfait cup, layer half of the Greek yogurt.
- Top with half of the berries.
- Sprinkle half of the granola.
- Repeat the layering with the remaining yogurt, berries, and granola.
- Drizzle with honey (if using) and sprinkle with cinnamon (if using).
- Enjoy immediately!

Nutritional Information (per serving):

- Calories: 250
- Fat: 5g
- Saturated fat: 2g
- Carbohydrates: 35g
- Fiber: 5g
- Sugar: 15g (including natural sugars from fruit)
- Protein: 20g
- Sodium: 150mg

Tips:
- Get creative with your berries! Use what's in season or mix and match your favorites.
- Choose a low-sugar granola to keep the overall sugar content moderate.
- Substitute honey with another natural sweetener like stevia or monk fruit extract if you prefer.
- Add a dollop of nut butter for extra protein and healthy

Scrambled Eggs with Spinach & Toast:

Ingredients (for 1 serving):
- 2 large eggs
- 1 tablespoon milk (your choice of dairy or non-dairy)
- 1/4 cup chopped spinach
- 1/4 teaspoon olive oil
- Salt and pepper to taste
- 1 slice of whole-wheat toast

Optional toppings
- Chopped avocado
- Sliced tomato
- Grated cheese
- Hot sauce

Instructions:

- In a small bowl, whisk together the eggs and milk until well combined.
- Heat the olive oil in a non-stick pan over medium heat.
- Add the spinach and saute for 1-2 minutes, until wilted.
- Pour in the egg mixture and cook, stirring occasionally, until scrambled to your desired consistency.
- Season with salt and pepper to taste.
- While the eggs are cooking, toast your bread to your desired level of crispness.
- Plate your scrambled eggs and top with your chosen toppings.
- Enjoy your delicious and nutritious breakfast!

Nutrition Information (per serving):
- Calories: 240
- Fat: 12g
- Saturated Fat: 2g
- Cholesterol: 140mg
- Sodium: 230mg
- Carbohydrates: 22g
- Fiber: 2g
- Sugar: 1g
- Protein: 14g

Tips:
- For a fluffier omelet-style scramble, cook the eggs until they are almost set, then fold them in half.
- Add other vegetables to your liking, such as mushrooms, onions, or bell peppers.
- Use a silicone spatula to easily fold and scramble the eggs.
- Adjust the amount of spinach and toppings to your liking.

Overnight Oats with Chia Seeds & Fruit:

Ingredients (for 1 serving):
- 1/2 cup rolled oats (old-fashioned or quick-cooking)
- 1/4 cup chia seeds
- 1 cup milk (unsweetened almond milk, cow's milk, soy milk, etc.)
- 1/4 cup chopped fruit (berries, banana, mango, etc.)
- 1 tablespoon nuts or seeds (almonds, walnuts, pumpkin seeds, etc.)
- Optional: 1 teaspoon honey, maple syrup, or sweetener of choice

Instructions:
- In a jar or container with a lid, combine the rolled oats, chia seeds, milk, and any sweeteners you're using. Stir well to ensure everything is combined.
- Cover the jar and refrigerate for at least 4 hours, or overnight.
- In the morning, stir the oats again and top with your chosen fruit and nuts or seeds. Enjoy!

Nutrition Information (per serving):
- Calories: Approximately 300-350 (depending on ingredients used)
- Carbohydrates: 40-50 grams
- Protein: 10-15 grams
- Fat: 10-15 grams
- Fiber: 5-10 grams

- Sugar: 5-10 grams (depending on fruit and sweetener used)

Tips:
- You can customize this recipe with different types of milk, fruits, nuts, and seeds.

- Add spices like cinnamon or nutmeg for extra flavor.
- If you prefer a thicker mixture, use less milk.
- If you like it sweeter, add more fruit or a bit more sweetener.
- Prepare a batch of overnight oats on the weekend for easy grab-and-go breakfasts throughout the week

Banana Smoothie with Spinach & Nut Butter:

Ingredients:
- 1 frozen ripe banana
- 1 cup unsweetened almond milk (or milk of your choice)
- 1/2 cup fresh spinach
- 2 tablespoons almond butter (or nut butter of your choice)
- 1/2 teaspoon ground cinnamon (optional)
- 1/4 cup ice cubes (optional)

Instructions:
- Combine all ingredients in a blender and blend until smooth and creamy. Add more almond milk or water if needed to reach desired consistency.
- Pour into a glass and enjoy!

Nutrition Information (per serving):
- Calories: 250
- Fat: 14g (2g saturated)
- Carbohydrates: 32g (12g sugar, 6g fiber)
- Protein: 9g
- Sodium: 130mg
- Potassium: 490 mg
- Calcium: 230mg
- Vitamin A: 4% Daily Value
- Vitamin C: 14% Daily Value
- Iron: 8% Daily Value

Tips:
- Use frozen bananas for a thicker smoothie.
- Add in other fruits like berries, mango, or pineapple for additional flavor and nutrients.
- If you don't have spinach, you can use kale or another leafy green.
- Substitute almond butter with any nut butter you prefer, like peanut butter or cashew butter.
- Add a scoop of protein powder for an extra protein boost.
- Garnish your smoothie with a sprinkle of chia seeds, nuts, or granola for added texture and crunch.

Cottage Cheese Toast with Sliced Tomatoes & Herbs:.

Ingredients:
- 1 slice whole-wheat bread
- 1/4 cup ricotta cheese
- 1/2 medium tomato, thinly sliced
- 1/4 cup fresh basil leaves, chopped (or other herb of your choice)
- Pinch of salt and black pepper
- 1 tablespoon extra virgin olive oil (optional)

Instructions:
- Toast the whole-wheat bread until golden brown.
- Spread the ricotta cheese evenly over the toast.
- Arrange the sliced tomatoes on top of the ricotta cheese.
- Sprinkle with chopped basil and season with salt and pepper to taste.
- Drizzle with olive oil, if desired.

Nutrition information per serving (without olive oil):
- Calories: 240
- Carbohydrates: 34 g
- Fat: 9 g
- Protein: 13 g
- Fiber: 3 g
- Sugar: 5 g
- Sodium: 300 mg

Tips:
- For a richer flavor, use toasted nuts or seeds instead of herbs.
- Try different types of ricotta cheese, like whole milk or part-skim ricotta.
- If you don't have fresh herbs, you can use dried herbs instead.
- Add a drizzle of balsamic vinegar for a tangy twist.

Whole-Wheat English Muffins with Avocado & Poached Egg:.

Ingredients (for 1 serving):
- 1 whole-wheat English muffin
- 1/2 ripe avocado, sliced
- 1 large egg
- 1 tablespoon white vinegar
- 1/2 teaspoon kosher salt
- Freshly ground black pepper, to taste
- Optional: Lemon juice, chili flakes, hot sauce

Instructions:
- Toast the English muffin: Using a toaster or oven, toast the English muffin to your desired level of crispness.
- Prepare the avocado: Slice the avocado in half, remove the pit, and carefully slice the flesh into thin pieces.
- Poach the egg: Fill a small saucepan with 3-4 inches of water and bring to a gentle simmer. Add the vinegar and stir to create a whirlpool effect. Crack the egg into a small bowl and gently slide it into the center of the simmering water. Cook for 3-4 minutes, until the white is set and the yolk is still runny.
- Assemble the breakfast: Place the toasted English muffin on a plate. Top with the avocado slices and season with a pinch of salt and pepper. Gently transfer the poached

egg onto the avocado and sprinkle with more salt and pepper, if desired.
- Enjoy! Drizzle with a squeeze of lemon juice, chili flakes, or hot sauce for additional flavor (optional).

Nutritional Information (per serving):
- Calories: 340
- Fat: 17g (2g saturated)
- Carbohydrates: 44g (5g fiber)
- Protein: 14g
- Sodium: 380mg
- Cholesterol: 215mg

Tips:
- For a smoother avocado spread, mash it slightly before topping the English muffin.
- If you don't have white vinegar, you can use cider vinegar or lemon juice instead.
- To make the poaching process easier, crack the egg into a small ramekin or dish before sliding it into the water.
- You can adjust the level of salt and pepper to your taste.
- Feel free to get creative with additional toppings! Sliced tomatoes, red onion, or fresh herbs can be added for extra flavor.

Chia Seed Pudding with Almond Milk & Fruit:.
Ingredients (for 1 serving):
- 2 tablespoons chia seeds
- 1/2 cup unsweetened almond milk
- 1/4 cup plain Greek yogurt (optional)
- 1/4 teaspoon vanilla extract (optional)
- 1/4 cup fresh or frozen berries (your choice)
- 1/4 cup sliced banana, apple, or mango (optional)
- 1/2 tablespoon chopped nuts or seeds (optional)
- Honey or maple syrup (optional, to taste)

Instructions:
- In a small bowl or jar, combine chia seeds, almond milk, Greek yogurt (if using), and vanilla extract (if using). Stir well and let sit for at least 30 minutes, or until the chia seeds have thickened and pudding is set.
- While the pudding is setting, prepare your fruit. Wash and slice berries, or chop banana, apple, or mango (if using).
- Once the pudding is set, divide it into a serving bowl or container. Top with your chosen fruit, chopped nuts or seeds (if using), and drizzle with honey or maple syrup (if using and desired).

Nutrition Information (per serving):
- Calories: 240
- Carbohydrates: 26g (includes 5g of fiber)
- Protein: 10g
- Fat: 8g (includes 1g saturated fat)
- Sodium: 40mg
- Sugar: 14g (includes natural sugars from fruit)

Tips:
- You can use any type of milk you like, such as cow's milk, coconut milk, or soy milk.
- Add a pinch of cinnamon or nutmeg to the pudding for extra flavor.

- If you prefer a sweeter pudding, add a tablespoon of honey or maple syrup before letting it set.
- Get creative with your toppings! Try other fruits like pineapple, kiwi, or peaches. You can also add granola, nut butter, or coconut flakes.
- This pudding can be stored in the refrigerator for up to 3 days.

Breakfast Burrito with Scrambled Eggs & Veggies:.

Ingredients:
- 1 large egg
- 1 tablespoon milk (optional)
- 1/4 teaspoon olive oil
- 1/4 cup chopped bell pepper (any color)
- 1/4 cup chopped onion
- 1/4 cup chopped spinach
- 1/4 cup cooked black beans, rinsed and drained (optional)
- 1/4 cup shredded cheese (cheddar, Monterey Jack, or your favorite)
- 1 whole-wheat tortilla

Instructions:
- In a small bowl, whisk together the egg and milk (if using). Set aside.
- Heat the olive oil in a small pan over medium heat. Add the bell pepper and onion, and cook until softened, about 5 minutes.
- Add the spinach and cook until wilted, about 1 minute.
- Push the vegetables to one side of the pan, and pour in the egg mixture. Scramble the eggs until cooked through.

- Add the black beans (if using) and stir to combine.
- Warm the tortilla in a dry skillet or microwave until pliable.
- Spread the cheese on the tortilla, then top with the scrambled eggs and vegetables.
- Roll up the tortilla, tucking in the ends.
- Enjoy immediately!

Nutrition Information (per serving):
- Calories: 320
- Fat: 14g (2g saturated)
- Carbohydrates: 36g (5g fiber, 7g sugar)
- Protein: 18g
- Sodium: 300mg (adjust depending on cheese and black beans used)

Tips:
- You can add other vegetables to the filling, such as mushrooms, zucchini, or tomatoes.
- Use pre-cooked black beans for even faster preparation.

- If you don't have a whole-wheat tortilla, you can use a smaller corn tortilla or even a low-carb wrap.

- Get creative with different cheeses and salsa!

Smoothie Bowl with Greek Yogurt, Granola & Nuts:.

Ingredients (one serving):
- ½ cup plain Greek yogurt (2% fat)
- ½ cup frozen berries (mixed or your favorite)
- ¼ cup unsweetened almond milk
- ¼ cup granola (low-sugar)
- ¼ cup mixed nuts and seeds (almonds, walnuts, pumpkin seeds, sunflower seeds)
- ¼ teaspoon chia seeds
- Optional toppings: fresh berries, a drizzle of honey, shredded coconut, cinnamon

Instructions:
- Blend the Greek yogurt, frozen berries, and almond milk in a blender until smooth and creamy.
- Pour the smoothie into a bowl.
- Top with granola, nuts and seeds, chia seeds, and any optional toppings you like.
- Enjoy your delicious and nutritious smoothie bowl!

Nutrition Information (per serving):
Calories: 350
- Fat: 15g (monounsaturated & polyunsaturated)
- Carbohydrates: 45g (fiber: 7g)
- Protein: 20g
- Sugar: 15g (naturally occurring from fruit)
- Sodium: 150mg

Tips:
- Use frozen bananas instead of berries for a thicker smoothie bowl.
- Add a scoop of protein powder if you need an extra boost.
- Get creative with your toppings! Try different fruits, nuts, seeds, and even a drizzle of nut butter.
- Make a double batch and store the extra smoothie in a sealed container in the fridge for a quick breakfast or snack later.

Baked Sweet Potato Toast with Toasted Nuts & Honey:.

Ingredients (for 2 servings):
- 1 large sweet potato
- 1 tablespoon olive oil
- Salt and pepper to taste
- 1/4 cup nuts of your choice (almonds, walnuts, pecans, etc.)
- 2 tablespoons honey (optional)
- 2 tablespoons ricotta cheese (optional)
- Fresh herbs like basil or thyme (optional)

Instructions:
- Preheat the oven to 400°F (200°C).

- Wash and dry the sweet potato. Slice it lengthwise into thick slabs (about 1/2 inch thick).
- Brush both sides of the sweet potato slices with olive oil. Season generously with salt and pepper.
- Arrange the sweet potato slices on a baking sheet in a single layer. Bake for 20-25 minutes, or until tender and lightly browned.
- While the sweet potato is baking, toast the nuts in a dry skillet over medium heat for 3-5 minutes, until fragrant and lightly browned. Watch them closely to avoid burning.
- Once the sweet potato is done, assemble the toast. Divide the ricotta cheese (if using) between the two slices. Top with toasted nuts and a drizzle of honey (if using). Garnish with fresh herbs (if using).

Nutrition Information per Serving (without ricotta or honey):
- Calories: 200
- Fat: 8g
- Carbohydrates: 35g
- Fiber: 4g
- Protein: 4g
- Sugar: 6g

Tips;
- You can experiment with different toppings for your sweet potato toast. Try mashed avocado, sliced tomatoes, or crumbled feta cheese.
- If you're watching your sugar intake, you can skip the honey or use a smaller amount.
- Leftover sweet potato toast can be stored in the refrigerator for up to 3 days. Reheat in the oven or toaster oven before serving

Quick & Convenient:

Hard-boiled Eggs with Whole-Wheat Toast & Avocado:

Ingredients (for 1 serving):
- 2 large eggs
- 1 slice whole-wheat toast
- 1/2 ripe avocado, sliced
- Sea salt and black pepper to taste
- Optional: Everything bagel seasoning, red pepper flakes, cilantro

Instructions:
- Hard-boil the eggs: Place the eggs in a saucepan and cover with cold water. Bring to a boil, then immediately remove from heat and cover the pan. Let the eggs sit for 10 minutes, then drain and cool under cold running water. Peel and set aside.
- Toast the bread: Toast the whole-wheat bread to your desired doneness.
- Assemble the meal: Spread the avocado slices on the toast. Slice the hard-boiled eggs and arrange them on top of the avocado. Season with sea salt and black pepper to taste.

- Optional toppings: Sprinkle with everything bagel seasoning, red pepper flakes, or chopped cilantro for additional flavor.

Nutrition Information (per serving):
- Calories: 330
- Fat: 20g (unsaturated)
- Carbohydrates: 25g (fiber: 5g)
- Protein: 15g
- Sodium: 300mg
- Sugar: 1g

Tips:
- Feel free to adjust the amount of avocado and toast based on your hunger level.
- You can use scrambled, poached, or fried eggs instead of hard-boiled eggs.
- This recipe is a good source of healthy fats, fiber, and protein, making it a balanced and satisfying breakfast option.

Whole-wheat Waffles with Greek Yogurt & Berries:.

Ingredients:
- 1 cup whole-wheat flour
- 1/2 cup all-purpose flour (can substitute almond flour for a gluten-free option)
- 2 teaspoons baking powder
- 1/4 teaspoon salt
- 1 1/2 cups milk (can use low-fat or plant-based milk)
- 1 egg
- 1 tablespoon vegetable oil
- 1 teaspoon vanilla extract
- 1/4 cup chopped nuts (optional)
- 1/2 cup Greek yogurt
- 1 cup fresh berries of your choice
- Maple syrup or honey (optional)

Instructions:
- Preheat your waffle iron according to the manufacturer's instructions.
- In a large bowl, whisk together the dry ingredients: whole-wheat flour, all-purpose flour, baking powder, and salt.
- In a separate bowl, whisk together the wet ingredients: milk, egg, vegetable oil, and vanilla extract.
- Pour the wet ingredients into the dry ingredients and mix until just combined. Do not overmix.
- Fold in the chopped nuts (optional) and any additional mix-ins you like, such as chocolate chips or dried fruit.
- Pour batter onto your preheated waffle iron and cook until golden brown and crispy, about 4-5 minutes per waffle.
- While waffles cook, prepare your toppings. Place Greek yogurt in a bowl and top with fresh berries.
- Serve waffles warm with a dollop of Greek yogurt and fresh berries. Drizzle with maple syrup or honey (optional) for added sweetness.

Nutritional Information (per serving):
- Calories: 350
- Carbohydrates: 45g
- Fiber: 4g

- Protein: 15g
- Fat: 15g
- Sugar: 10g (including natural sugars from fruit)

Tips:

- For a thicker batter, add a few tablespoons of rolled oats or almond flour.

.

- Make the waffles ahead of time and store them in the refrigerator for up to 3 days. Reheat in a toaster or oven before serving.
- This recipe is easily doubled or tripled if you need to feed a crowd.
- Get creative with your toppings! Try different types of yogurt, berries, nuts, seeds, or even crumbled tofu for a vegan option

Nut Butter & Banana Sandwich on Whole-Wheat Bread:

Ingredients (for 1 serving):

- 2 slices whole-wheat bread
- 2 tablespoons nut butter (almond, peanut, cashew, etc.)
- 1 medium banana, peeled and sliced
- Optional: pinch of cinnamon, sliced nuts, chia seeds

Instructions:

- Toast the bread to your desired level of crispness.
- Spread one tablespoon of nut butter on each slice of toast.
- Arrange banana slices on top of the nut butter.
- Sprinkle with cinnamon, sliced nuts, or chia seeds, if desired.

Nutrition Information (per serving):

- Calories: 350-400 (depending on the type of nut butter used)
- Fat: 15-20g
- Carbohydrates: 40-50g
- Protein: 5-10g
- Fiber: 5-10g
- Sugar: 10-15g
- Sodium: 150-200mg (depending on the type of nut butter used)

Tips:

- Use an unsweetened nut butter for a lower-sugar option.
- Add a handful of spinach or other leafy greens for extra nutrients.
- Drizzle with honey or maple syrup for a touch of sweetness.
- Cut the sandwich into bite-sized pieces for a fun and portable sna

Protein Bar with Fruit & Greek Yogurt

Ingredients (for 1 serving):

- 1 protein bar (choose one with at least 10g protein and minimal added sugar)

- 1/2 cup plain Greek yogurt (2% fat or non-fat)
- 1/2 cup chopped fresh fruit (berries, apple, banana, etc.)
- 1/4 cup granola (optional)
- Handful of nuts or seeds (optional)

Instructions:
- Crumble the protein bar into a bowl.
- Add the Greek yogurt and stir to combine.
- Top with your chosen chopped fruit.
- If desired, sprinkle with granola and nuts or seeds for added texture and nutrients.

Nutrition Information (per serving):
- Calories: Approximately 300-400 (depending on chosen ingredients)

- Protein: 20-25g
- Fat: 5-10g
- Carbohydrates: 30-40g
- Fiber: 3-5g
- Sugar: 10-15g (depending on added sugar in protein bar and fruit)

Tips:
- Choose a protein bar with minimal added sugar and focus on natural ingredients.
- For a vegan option, use a plant-based protein bar and dairy-free yogurt.
- If you like it colder, mix in a frozen banana or some frozen berries for a smoothie-like consistency.
- Get creative with your toppings! You can add honey, cinnamon, chia seeds, or anything else you like for extra flavor and nutrients.

Trail Mix with Yogurt & Honey: A Nourishing Grab-and-Go Breakfast

Ingredients:
- For the trail mix:
- 1/2 cup unsalted almonds
- 1/4 cup walnuts
- 1/4 cup dried cranberries
- 1/4 cup dried chopped mango
- 1/4 cup pumpkin seeds
- 1/4 cup sunflower seeds
- 1 tablespoon unsweetened shredded coconut
- For the serving:
- 1 cup plain Greek yogurt (2% or non-fat)
- 1 tablespoon honey
- 1/4 cup trail mix

Instructions:
- Preheat the oven to 350°F (175°C). Spread the nuts and seeds on a baking sheet and toast for 5-7 minutes, or until slightly golden brown. Let cool slightly.
- In a large bowl, combine the cooled nuts and seeds with the dried fruit and coconut. Mix well.
- To assemble the breakfast parfait, divide the yogurt between two bowls. Drizzle each bowl with honey and top with 1/4 cup of the trail mix.
- Enjoy!

Nutrition Information (per serving):
- Calories: 350
- Fat: 15g (monounsaturated and polyunsaturated)
- Carbohydrates: 35g (fiber: 5g)
- Protein: 15g
- Sugar: 18g (including natural sugars from fruit and honey)
- Sodium: 130mg

Tips:
- Feel free to customize the trail mix to your liking! Add other nuts, seeds, dried fruit, or dark chocolate chips.
- Use portion control containers to pre-measure the trail mix for grab-and-go convenience.
- Substitute the honey with maple syrup or a splash of fruit juice for a different flavor.
- Make it vegan! Use plant-based yogurt and substitute honey with agave syrup or another vegan sweetener.

Edamame Pods with Sea Salt & Sriracha:.

Ingredients:
- 1/2 cup frozen edamame pods, thawed
- 1/2 teaspoon sea salt
- Pinch of sriracha, to taste (optional)
- Lime wedge (optional)

Instructions:
- Thaw the edamame: If using frozen edamame, thaw them completely in the microwave or under cold running water. You can also steam them for 2-3 minutes until warmed through.
- Season with salt & sriracha: Place the thawed edamame in a bowl and sprinkle with sea salt. Add a pinch of sriracha, if desired, and toss to coat evenly.
- Serve immediately: Enjoy the edamame pods as a snack or light appetizer. Squeeze a lime wedge over them for an extra bit of zest, if desired.

Nutrition Information (per serving):
- Calories: 80
- Fat: 3g
- Saturated Fat: 0.5g
- Cholesterol: 0mg
- Sodium: 130mg (depending on sea salt brand)
- Carbohydrates: 10g
- Fiber: 2g
- Sugar: 2g
- Protein: 7g

Tips:
- For a spicier kick, add a few dashes of sriracha or use chili flakes instead.
- Serve with a dipping sauce like hummus or Greek yogurt for additional flavor and protein.
- Roast the edamame pods in the oven for 10-15 minutes at 400°F for a crispier texture.

- Add chopped herbs like cilantro or parsley for a fresh twis

Cottage Cheese with Sliced Cucumbers & Herbs:.

Ingredients (for 1 serving):

- 1/2 cup (125g) full-fat cottage cheese
- 1/2 cucumber, thinly sliced
- 1/4 cup chopped fresh herbs (dill, chives, parsley, or a combination)
- 1 tablespoon olive oil
- 1/4 teaspoon freshly squeezed lemon juice (optional)
- Salt and black pepper to taste

Nutritional Information (per serving):

- Calories: 210
- Carbohydrates: 12g (3g fiber, 6g sugar)
- Protein: 20g
- Fat: 12g (6g saturated)
- Sodium: 380mg
- Cholesterol: 40mg

Instructions:

- In a small bowl, combine the cottage cheese, cucumber slices, and chopped herbs. Stir gently to combine.
- Drizzle with olive oil and lemon juice (if using). Season with salt and pepper to taste.
- Serve immediately on its own or with whole-wheat crackers or toast.

Tips:

- Use any type of fresh herbs you like! Mint, basil, and oregano are also good options.
- For a creamier consistency, you can blend the cottage cheese with a splash of milk or yogurt.
- Add a sprinkle of nuts or seeds for extra crunch and protein.
- This recipe is easily doubled or tripled if you need to feed more people.
- You can also make this in advance and store it in an airtight container in the refrigerator for up to 3 days.

Avocado Toast with Everything Bagel Seasoning:.

Ingredients (for 1 serving):

- 1 slice whole-wheat toast
- 1/4 ripe avocado
- 1 tablespoon extra virgin olive oil
- Everything Bagel Seasoning (to taste)
- Pinch of flaky sea salt (optional)
- Additional toppings (optional): sliced tomato, red onion, smoked salmon, crumbled feta cheese, microgreens

Instructions:

- Toast the whole-wheat bread to your desired doneness.
- While the toast is warm, mash the avocado with a fork until creamy.

- Spread the avocado mash onto the toasted bread.
- Drizzle the avocado with olive oil and sprinkle generously with Everything Bagel Seasoning.
- Optionally, add a pinch of flaky sea salt for extra flavor.
- Get creative with your toppings! Add sliced tomato, red onion, smoked salmon, crumbled feta cheese, microgreens, or any other combination you enjoy.

Nutrition Information (per serving):
- Calories: 240
- Fat: 17g (monounsaturated) Carbohydrates: 24g (fiber 4g)

- Protein: 8g
- Sodium: 280mg (adjust with low-sodium Everything Bagel Seasoning if needed)

Tips:
- Use ripe avocados for the best flavor and texture.
- To speed up the avocado mashing process, score the avocado flesh before scooping it out.
- Make it a complete meal by adding a side of hard-boiled eggs, Greek yogurt with fruit, or a fresh fruit salad.
- Store leftover avocado mash in an airtight container in the refrigerator for up to 2 days.

Greek Yogurt with Chia Seeds & Honey:

Ingredients (for 1 serving):
- 1 cup (240g) plain Greek yogurt (2% fat or non-fat)
- 2 tablespoons chia seeds
- 1 tablespoon honey
- 1/4 cup (30g) fresh berries (optional)
- 1/4 cup (25g) chopped nuts (optional)

Instructions:
- In a bowl, combine the Greek yogurt, chia seeds, and honey. Mix well until the chia seeds are evenly distributed.
- Let the mixture sit for 5 minutes to allow the chia seeds to plump up.
- Top the yogurt with fresh berries and chopped nuts, if desired.
- Enjoy immediately or refrigerate for a colder breakfast.

Nutrition Information (per serving):
- Calories: 220
- Carbohydrates: 25g (including 4g sugar)
- Fat: 6g (1g saturated)
- Protein: 18g
- Fiber: 5g

Tips:
- Use any type of Greek yogurt you like, but choose plain yogurt for optimal blood sugar control.
- Feel free to adjust the amount of honey to your sweetness preference.
- You can substitute berries with other fruits like chopped apple, mango, or pineapple.
- Adding nuts provides healthy fats and extra protein.

Fruit Salad with Coconut Yogurt & Granola:.

Ingredients (for 1 serving):
- 1/2 cup mixed berries (e.g., strawberries, blueberries, raspberries)
- 1/4 cup chopped kiwi
- 1/4 cup chopped pineapple
- 1/4 cup chopped red grapes
- 1/4 cup plain coconut yogurt
- 1/4 cup mixed nuts and seeds (almonds, walnuts, sunflower seeds, pumpkin seeds)
- 1/4 cup granola (choose a low-sugar option)
- 1/4 teaspoon shredded coconut (optional)
- 1 tablespoon honey or maple syrup (optional)

Instructions:
- Wash and chop all fruits into bite-sized pieces.
- In a bowl, combine the berries, kiwi, pineapple, and grapes.
- In a separate bowl, stir together the coconut yogurt and honey or maple syrup, if using.
- Divide the fruit salad between two bowls or one serving dish.
- Top each bowl with the coconut yogurt mixture, granola, nuts and seeds, and shredded coconut, if using.

Nutrition Information (per serving):
- Calories: 350
- Fat: 15g (4g saturated)
- Carbohydrates: 50g (10g sugar)
- Fiber: 5g
- Protein: 10g
- Sodium: 100mg

Tips:
- Feel free to customize this recipe with your favorite fruits and nuts.
- For a thicker yogurt mixture, you can strain the coconut yogurt overnight.
- Add a sprinkle of cinnamon or nutmeg for extra flavor.
- If you don't have granola, you can use rolled oats or puffed quinoa.
- This recipe is easily doubled or tripled to serve a crowd.

Lunch (Delicious & Nutritious Midday Meals)

Salads with Flair:

Mediterranean Chickpea Salad:.

Ingredients:

- 1 (15 oz) can chickpeas, drained and rinsed
- 1 cup cherry tomatoes, halved
- 1/2 large cucumber, diced
- 1/4 red onion, finely diced
- 1/4 cup crumbled feta cheese
- 1/4 cup chopped fresh parsley
- 2 tablespoons olive oil
- 1 tablespoon lemon juice
- 1 teaspoon dried oregano
- 1/2 teaspoon salt
- 1/4 teaspoon black pepper
- Optional: Kalamata olives, sliced

Instructions:

- In a large bowl, combine the chickpeas, tomatoes, cucumber, red onion, feta cheese, and parsley.
- In a separate small bowl, whisk together the olive oil, lemon juice, oregano, salt, and pepper.
- Pour the dressing over the chickpea mixture and toss to combine.
- Add Kalamata olives, if using, and serve chilled.

Nutrition per Serving (based on 6 servings):

- Calories: 220
- Fat: 9 grams
- Saturated Fat: 1 gram
- Cholesterol: 5 mg
- Sodium: 230 mg
- Carbohydrates: 27 grams
- Fiber: 4 grams
- Sugar: 5 grams
- Protein: 10 grams

Tips:

- For a vegan option, omit the feta cheese and use a plant-based milk (such as almond milk) in the dressing.
- Add other vegetables, such as chopped bell peppers or chopped celery, for additional flavor and texture.
- Serve the salad on a bed of lettuce or with whole-wheat pita bread for a more filling meal.
- Leftovers can be stored in an airtight container in the refrigerator for up to 3 days.

Southwest Fiesta Salad:.

Ingredients (for 4 servings):

- 1 head romaine lettuce, chopped
- 1 cup cooked black beans, rinsed and drained
- 1 cup cooked corn kernels, fresh or frozen
- 1/2 cup diced red bell pepper
- 1/2 cup diced red onion
- 1 ripe avocado, diced
- 1/2 cup chopped fresh cilantro
- 4 small boneless, skinless chicken breasts, grilled or baked and sliced

- 1/4 cup crumbled queso fresco cheese (optional)
- 1/4 cup lime juice
- 2 tablespoons olive oil
- 1 tablespoon honey
- 1 teaspoon chili powder
- 1/2 teaspoon cumin
- 1/4 teaspoon garlic powder
- Salt and pepper to taste

Instructions:
- In a large bowl, combine the chopped romaine lettuce, black beans, corn, bell pepper, red onion, avocado, and cilantro.
- In a separate bowl, whisk together the lime juice, olive oil, honey, chili powder, cumin, and garlic powder. Season with salt and pepper to taste.
- Pour the dressing over the salad and toss to coat.
- Top the salad with the sliced chicken and queso fresco cheese (optional).
- Serve immediately and enjoy!

Nutrition per serving (approximate):
- Calories: 420
- Fat: 14g
- Saturated fat: 2g
- Cholesterol: 75mg
- Sodium: 300mg
- Carbohydrates: 44g
- Fiber: 8g
- Sugar: 10g
- Protein: 32g

Tips:
- You can adjust the spiciness of the dressing to your liking by adding more or less chili powder.
- For a vegetarian option, omit the chicken and add another cup of black beans or another protein source like tofu or tempeh.
- Leftovers can be stored in an airtight container in the refrigerator for up to 2 days. However, the avocado may brown slightly.

I hope you enjoy this delicious and nutritious Southwest Fiesta Salad!

Quinoa & Grilled Chicken Salad:

Ingredients (Serves 4):
- 1 cup quinoa, rinsed
- 2 boneless, skinless chicken breasts
- 1 tablespoon olive oil
- 1/2 teaspoon salt
- 1/4 teaspoon black pepper
- 2 cups mixed greens
- 1 cup cherry tomatoes, halved
- 1/2 cup cucumber, chopped
- 1/4 cup red onion, thinly sliced
- 1/4 cup crumbled feta cheese
- 1/4 cup chopped fresh parsley

Balsamic Vinaigrette:
- 2 tablespoons olive oil
- 1 tablespoon balsamic vinegar
- 1 teaspoon Dijon mustard
- 1/2 teaspoon honey
- Salt and pepper to taste

Instructions:

- Cook the quinoa: In a saucepan, combine the quinoa with 2 cups of water. Bring to a boil, then reduce heat, cover, and simmer for 15 minutes or until fluffy. Remove from heat and let cool slightly.
- Marinate the chicken: In a small bowl, whisk together the olive oil, salt, and pepper. Place the chicken breasts in the marinade and let sit for at least 15 minutes.
- Grill the chicken: Preheat your grill to medium-high heat. Grill the chicken breasts for 5-7 minutes per side, or until cooked through. Let cool slightly, then slice or shred the chicken.
- Assemble the salad: In a large bowl, combine the cooled quinoa, mixed greens, cherry tomatoes, cucumber, red onion, and feta cheese. Add the sliced or shredded chicken and parsley.
- Make the vinaigrette: In a separate bowl, whisk together the olive oil, balsamic vinegar, Dijon mustard, honey, salt, and pepper.
- Dress the salad: Drizzle the salad with the balsamic vinaigrette and toss to coat.

Nutrition per Serving (Approximate):
- Calories: 400
- Fat: 15g
- Carbohydrates: 45g
- Fiber: 5g
- Protein: 30g
- Sodium: 350mg

Tips:
- For a vegetarian option, substitute grilled tofu or tempeh for the chicken.
- Add other vegetables to your liking, such as bell peppers, corn, or avocado.
- Make the vinaigrette ahead of time and store it in the refrigerator for up to a week.
- If you don't have a grill, you can cook the chicken in a pan on the stovetop.

Asian Noodle Salad with Peanut Dressing:

Ingredients (Serves 4)
For the salad:
- 12 ounces rice noodles (brown or white)
- 2 cups shredded vegetables (carrots, cucumbers, bell peppers, etc.)
- 1 cup chopped cooked chicken or tofu (optional)
- 1 cup chopped fresh herbs (cilantro, mint, basil)
- 1/2 cup chopped peanuts
- Sesame seeds, for garnishing

For the peanut dressing:
- 3 tablespoons creamy peanut butter
- 2 tablespoons soy sauce
- 1 tablespoon rice vinegar
- 1 tablespoon lime juice
- 1 teaspoon honey

- 1 teaspoon Sriracha (adjust to your spice preference)
- 1 clove garlic, minced
- 1 inch ginger, grated
- 1/4 cup water

Instructions:
- Cook the noodles: Follow the package instructions to cook the rice noodles. Once cooked, drain and rinse with cold water to stop the cooking process.
- Prepare the dressing: In a small bowl, whisk together the peanut butter, soy sauce, rice vinegar, lime juice, honey, Sriracha, garlic, and ginger. Gradually add water until you reach a desired consistency (thin enough to coat the noodles, but not watery).
- Assemble the salad: In a large bowl, combine the cooked noodles, shredded vegetables, cooked chicken or tofu (if using), herbs, and chopped peanuts. Pour the peanut dressing over the salad and toss to coat evenly.

- Serve: Garnish with additional sesame seeds and enjoy!

Nutrition per serving (approximate):
- Calories: 450
- Fat: 15g
- Saturated fat: 2g
- Cholesterol: 30mg
- Sodium: 450mg
- Carbohydrates: 60g
- Fiber: 5g
- Sugar: 10g
- Protein: 20g

Tips:
- Feel free to customize the vegetables and protein to your preferences. Other options include shredded broccoli, snap peas, edamame, shrimp, or grilled salmon.
- For a vegan option, omit the chicken or tofu and use vegan peanut butter in the dressing.
- If you prefer a spicy salad, add more Sriracha to the dressing.
- Make this salad ahead of time for a quick and easy lunch option. Just store it in the fridge until you're ready to eat.

Soups for Every Season:

Creamy Tomato Bisque:

Ingredients:
- 2 tablespoons olive oil
- 1 large onion, chopped
- 3 cloves garlic, minced
- 1 teaspoon dried thyme
- 1/2 teaspoon dried oregano
- 28 oz (4 cans) fire-roasted diced tomatoes, undrained
- 4 cups vegetable broth
- 1 cup heavy cream (can substitute with unsweetened almond milk for a lighter option)
- 1/2 cup water (optional, adjust for desired consistency)
- Salt and freshly ground black pepper, to taste
- Fresh basil leaves, for garnish (optional)

Instructions:
- Heat olive oil in a large saucepan over medium heat. Add onion and cook until softened, about 5 minutes.
- Stir in garlic, thyme, and oregano. Cook for another minute until fragrant.
- Add the diced tomatoes and their juices. Bring to a simmer and cook for 15 minutes, stirring occasionally.
- Pour in the vegetable broth and bring to a boil. Reduce heat and simmer for 10 minutes.
- Using an immersion blender or in batches, carefully blend the soup until smooth and creamy.
- Stir in the heavy cream (or almond milk) and water (if using), and season with salt and pepper to taste.
- Serve hot, garnished with fresh basil leaves if desired.

Nutrition per Serving (based on 4 servings):
- Calories: 280
- Fat: 17g
- Saturated fat: 8g
- Cholesterol: 35mg
- Sodium: 430mg
- Carbohydrates: 21g
- Fiber: 3g
- Sugar: 12g
- Protein: 8g

Tips:
- For a richer flavor, roast the tomatoes before adding them to the soup. Simply place them on a baking sheet and drizzle with olive oil. Roast at 400°F for 20 minutes, or until softened and slightly blistered.
- You can substitute the heavy cream with full-fat coconut milk for a dairy-free and slightly tropical twist.
- Get creative with toppings! Croutons, crumbled goat cheese, pesto, or a drizzle of hot sauce can all add additional flavor and texture.
- Leftovers can be stored in an airtight container in the refrigerator for up to 3 days. Reheat gently on the stovetop or in the microwave

Spicy Lentil Stew:

Ingredients:(Serves 4)
- 1 tablespoon olive oil
- 1 large onion, diced
- 2 cloves garlic, minced
- 1 red bell pepper, diced
- 2 celery stalks, diced
- 2 carrots, diced
- 1 teaspoon ground cumin
- 1/2 teaspoon smoked paprika
- 1/4 teaspoon ground coriander
- 1/4 teaspoon chili powder (adjust to your spice preference)
- 1 (14.5 oz) can diced tomatoes, undrained
- 4 cups vegetable broth
- 1 cup green lentils, rinsed
- 1/2 cup chopped fresh parsley, for garnish
- Salt and pepper to taste

Optional Toppings:
- Sour cream or plain yogurt
- Grated Parmesan cheese
- Chopped avocado
- Hot sauce

Instructions:
- Heat olive oil in a large pot or Dutch oven over medium heat. Add the onion and cook for 5 minutes, or until softened and translucent.
- Add the garlic, bell pepper, celery, and carrots, and cook for another 5 minutes, or until softened.
- Stir in the cumin, paprika, coriander, and chili powder, and cook for 1 minute, until fragrant.
- Add the diced tomatoes and vegetable broth, and bring to a boil.
- Stir in the lentils, reduce heat to low, cover, and simmer for 20-25 minutes, or until the lentils are tender.
- Season with salt and pepper to taste.
- Ladle the stew into bowls and garnish with chopped parsley. Serve with your favorite toppings, if desired.

Nutrition per Serving (approximate):
- Calories: 350
- Fat: 10g
- Saturated fat: 1.5g
- Cholesterol: 0mg
- Sodium: 350mg
- Carbohydrates: 45g
- Fiber: 10g
- Sugar: 5g
- Protein: 15g

Tips:
- You can use brown lentils instead of green lentils for a slightly different texture and flavor.
- Add other vegetables to the stew, such as zucchini, spinach, or kale.
- For a thicker stew, mash some of the lentils against the side of the pot with a fork.

Chilled Cucumber Gazpacho:

Ingredients (for 4 servings):

- 2 large cucumbers (peeled and chopped)
- 2 large ripe tomatoes (seeded and chopped)
- 1 red bell pepper (seeded and chopped)
- 1/2 onion (chopped)
- 2 garlic cloves (chopped)
- 1/2 cup fresh cilantro (chopped)
- 1/4 cup fresh basil (chopped)
- 2 tablespoons olive oil
- 2 tablespoons lemon juice
- 1/2 teaspoon salt
- 1/4 teaspoon black pepper
- Water (optional)
- Optional toppings: Chopped cucumber, tomato, red onion, fresh herbs, croutons, avocado

Instructions:

- Combine all ingredients except water and optional toppings in a blender. Blend until smooth and creamy.
- Taste and adjust seasoning as needed, adding more salt, pepper, lemon juice, or water for desired consistency.
- Chill the gazpacho in the refrigerator for at least 2 hours, or overnight for deeper flavor.
- Serve chilled in bowls, garnished with your desired toppings.

Nutrition per serving (approximate):

- Calories: 150
- Fat: 8g
- Protein: 3g
- Carbohydrates: 18g
- Fiber: 2g
- Sugar: 7g
- Vitamin A: 30%
- Vitamin C: 80%
- Potassium: 15%

Tips:

- Use a variety of colors for your bell peppers and tomatoes for an even more vibrant gazpacho.
- If you prefer a thinner soup, add some water until you reach your desired consistency.
- This gazpacho can be stored in the refrigerator for up to 3 days.
- Get creative with your toppings! Chopped avocado, croutons, and a drizzle of olive oil are delicious additions.

Black Bean Soup with Avocado Salsa.

Ingredients:

Soup:

- 1 tablespoon olive oil
- 1 onion, chopped
- 2 cloves garlic, minced
- 1 green bell pepper, chopped
- 1 red bell pepper, chopped
- 2 jalapeños, seeded and chopped (optional, for additional spice)
- 1 teaspoon ground cumin
- 1/2 teaspoon smoked paprika

- 1 (15-ounce) can diced tomatoes, undrained
- 4 cups vegetable broth
- 1 (15-ounce) can black beans, rinsed and drained
- 1 (14.5-ounce) can corn, drained
- Salt and pepper to taste

Avocado Salsa:
- 1 ripe avocado, diced
- 1/4 cup red onion, finely chopped
- 1/4 cup fresh cilantro, chopped
- 1 tablespoon lime juice
- Pinch of salt and pepper

Instructions:
- In a large pot over medium heat, heat olive oil. Add onion and cook until softened, about 5 minutes. Add garlic, bell peppers, and jalapeños (if using) and cook for another 2 minutes.
- Stir in cumin and paprika and cook for 30 seconds, until fragrant.
- Add diced tomatoes, vegetable broth, black beans, and corn. Bring to a boil, then reduce heat and simmer for 20 minutes, or until vegetables are tender.
- While the soup simmers, prepare the avocado salsa. In a small bowl, combine diced avocado, red onion, cilantro, lime juice, salt, and pepper. Stir gently to combine and set aside.
- After simmering, use an immersion blender or a blender to puree the soup partially, leaving some texture. Season with salt and pepper to taste.
- Ladle the soup into bowls and top with a generous dollop of avocado salsa.

Nutrition per Serving (based on 4 servings):
- Calories: 320
- Fat: 14g (2g saturated)
- Carbohydrates: 44g (5g fiber, 8g sugar)
- Protein: 15g
- Sodium: 530mg

Tips:
- Serve with brown rice or quinoa for a more filling meal.
- Add other toppings like chopped fresh tomatoes, sour cream, or cheese.
- For a dairy-free option, use coconut milk instead of broth.
- Leftovers can be stored in an airtight container in the refrigerator for up to 3 days.

Sandwiches Reinvented:

Grilled Portobello with Goat Cheese:

Ingredients:
- 1 large portobello mushroom
- 2 tablespoons olive oil
- 1/2 teaspoon dried oregano
- 1/4 teaspoon salt
- 1/4 teaspoon black pepper
- 2 ounces goat cheese
- 1/4 cup arugula
- 1 tablespoon balsamic glaze (optional)

Instructions:
- Preheat the grill to medium-high heat.
- Clean the portobello mushroom by gently wiping it with a damp paper towel. Remove the stem (you can chop it and grill it alongside the mushroom, if desired).
- In a small bowl, whisk together olive oil, oregano, salt, and pepper. Brush the mixture generously over both sides of the portobello mushroom.
- Place the portobello mushroom on the preheated grill and cook for 3-4 minutes per side, or until tender and slightly charred.
- Remove the portobello from the grill and spread goat cheese evenly over the top.
- Top with arugula and drizzle with balsamic glaze, if desired.

Nutrition per serving:
- Calories: 240
- Fat: 18g
- Saturated fat: 5g
- Cholesterol: 30mg
- Sodium: 380mg
- Carbohydrates: 14g
- Fiber: 3g
- Sugar: 3g
- Protein: 10g

Tips:
- For a richer flavor, marinate the portobello mushroom in the olive oil and herb mixture for at least 30 minutes before grilling.
- Add other toppings to your liking, such as roasted vegetables, grilled onions, or chopped nuts.
- Serve the grilled portobello with a side salad or roasted vegetables for a complete meal.

Turkey & Cranberry Wraps:

Ingredients (for 4 wraps):
- 4 whole-wheat tortillas (8-inch diameter)
- 8 ounces thinly sliced deli turkey breast
- 1/2 cup cranberry sauce (whole berry preferred)
- 2 cups baby spinach
- 1/2 cup chopped pecans
- Salt and pepper to taste (optional)

Instructions:

- Spread 2 tablespoons of cranberry sauce evenly on each tortilla.
- Layer 2 ounces of sliced turkey breast over the cranberry sauce on each tortilla.
- Top each wrap with about 1/2 cup of baby spinach and sprinkle with 1/4 cup of chopped pecans.
- Season with salt and pepper to taste, if desired.
- Roll up the tortillas tightly and enjoy!

Nutrition per Serving (based on 1 wrap):

- Calories: 340
- Fat: 12g (1.5g saturated)
- Carbohydrates: 44g (5g fiber, 8g sugar)
- Protein: 22g
- Sodium: 480mg (adjust with low-sodium cranberry sauce)
- Cholesterol: 70mg

Tips:

- For a vegetarian option, replace the turkey with sliced avocado or tofu.
- Add crumbled feta cheese or goat cheese for an extra tangy flavor.
- For a warm wrap, heat the tortillas briefly in a dry pan or microwave before assembling.
- Serve with a side of cut fruits or yogurt for a complete and balanced meal.

Vegetarian Pita Pockets:

Ingredients (for 4 pita pockets):

- 2 whole-wheat pita breads
- 1/2 cup chopped red bell pepper
- 1/2 cup chopped zucchini
- 1/2 cup chopped red onion
- 1 tablespoon olive oil
- 1/2 teaspoon dried oregano
- 1/4 teaspoon salt
- 1/4 teaspoon black pepper
- 1/4 cup hummus
- 1/4 cup crumbled feta cheese
- 1/4 cup chopped spinach
- Optional: Drizzle of balsamic glaze or lemon juice

Instructions:

- Preheat the oven to 400°F (200°C). Line a baking sheet with parchment paper.
- Toss chopped red bell pepper, zucchini, and red onion with olive oil, oregano, salt, and black pepper. Spread evenly on the prepared baking sheet.
- Roast vegetables for 20-25 minutes, or until tender and slightly browned.
- While vegetables roast, warm the pita breads in a dry pan or microwave for about 30 seconds.
- Spread hummus evenly inside each pita pocket.
- Top with roasted vegetables, crumbled feta cheese, and chopped spinach.

- Drizzle with balsamic glaze or lemon juice, if desired.

Nutrition per serving (approximate):
- Calories: 300
- Fat: 10g
- Carbohydrates: 40g
- Fiber: 6g
- Protein: 15g
- Sodium: 350mg

Tips:

- Feel free to customize the vegetables! Try other options like broccoli, eggplant, or sweet potato.
- If you don't have hummus, you can use mashed avocado or a plant-based yogurt spread.
- Add some additional protein by mixing some chopped chickpeas or lentils into the hummus.
- For a touch of spice, add a pinch of red pepper flakes to the roasted vegetables.
- These pita pockets can be stored in an airtight container in the refrigerator for up to 2 days.

Tuna Salad Lettuce Wraps:

Ingredients (for 4 wraps):
- 2 cans (6 oz each) tuna packed in water, drained
- 1/2 cup chopped celery
- 1/4 cup chopped red onion
- 2 tablespoons chopped dill pickles
- 1 tablespoon mayonnaise
- 1 tablespoon Dijon mustard
- 1 teaspoon lemon juice
- 1/4 teaspoon salt
- 1/4 teaspoon black pepper
- 8 large romaine lettuce leaves, washed and patted dry

Instructions:
- In a medium bowl, flake the tuna with a fork. Add the chopped celery, red onion, dill pickles, mayonnaise, Dijon mustard, lemon juice, salt, and pepper. Stir well to combine.

- Wash and pat dry the romaine lettuce leaves.
- Divide the tuna salad evenly between the lettuce leaves. Wrap them tightly and enjoy!

Nutrition per serving (1 wrap):
- Calories: 160
- Fat: 8g
- Saturated Fat: 1g
- Cholesterol: 30mg
- Sodium: 280mg
- Carbohydrates: 4g
- Fiber: 1g
- Sugar: 1g
- Protein: 20g

Tips:

- For a lighter option, use Greek yogurt instead of mayonnaise.
- Add other chopped vegetables to the salad, such as bell peppers, cucumber, or carrots.
- Serve with avocado slices or a dollop of hummus for added flavor and nutrients.
- Get creative with your lettuce! Try using butter lettuce, bibb lettuce, or even collard greens for a different taste and texture.

One-Pan Wonders:

Sheet Pan Salmon with Veggies:

Ingredients:
- 2 salmon filets (6 oz each)
- 1 tablespoon olive oil
- 1/2 teaspoon sea salt
- 1/4 teaspoon black pepper
- 1 lemon, sliced
- 1 cup cherry tomatoes
- 1 cup broccoli florets
- 1/2 cup red onion, sliced
- 1/4 cup fresh parsley, chopped (optional)

Instructions:
- Preheat the oven to 400°F (200°C). Line a baking sheet with parchment paper.
- Place salmon fillets on the prepared baking sheet. Drizzle with olive oil and season with salt and pepper. Arrange lemon slices around the salmon.
- Scatter cherry tomatoes, broccoli florets, and red onion around the salmon, ensuring everything is in a single layer.
- Bake for 15-20 minutes, or until the salmon is cooked through and the vegetables are tender-crisp.
- Garnish with chopped parsley (optional) and serve immediately.

Nutrition per Serving (based on 1 serving):
- Calories: 450
- Fat: 25g
- Saturated Fat: 4g
- Cholesterol: 80mg
- Sodium: 450mg
- Carbohydrates: 15g
- Fiber: 2g
- Sugar: 7g
- Protein: 35g

Tips:
- You can substitute other vegetables for the ones listed in the recipe, such as asparagus, Brussels sprouts, or bell peppers.
- If you prefer your vegetables softer, you can pre-cook them for a few minutes before adding them to the baking sheet.
- To make a complete meal, add a side of quinoa or brown rice.
- Feel free to experiment with different herbs and spices to personalize the flavor.

Lemon Chicken with Asparagus:

Ingredients (Serves 4):
- 4 boneless, skinless chicken breasts (approximately 150g each)
- 1 tablespoon olive oil
- 1/2 teaspoon salt
- 1/4 teaspoon black pepper
- 1/2 teaspoon garlic powder
- 1/4 teaspoon paprika (optional)
- 1 tablespoon lemon zest
- 2 tablespoons fresh lemon juice
- 1/4 cup chicken broth

- 1 pound asparagus, trimmed and cut into 1-inch pieces
- Chopped fresh parsley, for garnish (optional)

Instructions:
- Preheat the oven to 400°F (200°C). Line a baking sheet with parchment paper.
- Pat the chicken breasts dry with paper towels. Season both sides with salt, pepper, garlic powder, and paprika (if using).
- Heat olive oil in a large oven-safe skillet over medium heat. Sear the chicken breasts for 2-3 minutes per side until golden brown.
- Remove the chicken from the pan and set aside on a plate.
- In the same skillet, add the lemon zest, lemon juice, and chicken broth. Bring to a simmer, scraping up any browned bits from the bottom of the pan.
- Add the asparagus to the pan and cook for 3-4 minutes, or until tender-crisp.
- Return the chicken breasts to the pan, spooning the sauce over them.
- Transfer the entire skillet to the preheated oven and bake for 15-20 minutes, or until the chicken is cooked through and the asparagus is tender.
- Garnish with chopped parsley, if desired, and serve immediately.

Nutrition per Serving (approximate):
- Calories: 350
- Fat: 15g
- Saturated fat: 3g
- Cholesterol: 80mg
- Sodium: 450mg
- Carbohydrates: 15g
- Fiber: 2g
- Sugar: 4g
- Protein: 40g

Tips:
- For a thicker sauce, mix 1 tablespoon of cornstarch with 2 tablespoons of cold water and stir it into the pan after adding the asparagus. Bring to a simmer until thickened.
- You can substitute chicken thighs for breasts for a richer flavor and juicier texture. Just adjust the cooking time, as thighs take longer to cook through.
- Feel free to add other vegetables to the pan, such as cherry tomatoes, bell peppers, or zucchini.
- Serve this dish with quinoa, brown rice, or roasted potatoes for a complete and satisfying meal

Spicy Shrimp Scampi with Linguine

Ingredients:
- 1 tablespoon olive oil
- 2 cloves garlic, minced
- 1/2 teaspoon red pepper flakes (adjust to your spice preference)
- 1/4 cup dry white wine
- 1/2 cup chicken broth
- 1 pound large shrimp, peeled and deveined
- 1/4 cup chopped fresh parsley

- Salt and freshly ground black pepper to taste
- 12 ounces linguine pasta
- Lemon wedges, for serving (optional)

Instructions:
- Heat olive oil in a large skillet over medium heat. Add garlic and chili flakes, and cook for 30 seconds, until fragrant.
- Pour in white wine and chicken broth, and bring to a simmer. Scrape up any browned bits from the bottom of the pan.
- Add shrimp and cook for 2-3 minutes per side, or until opaque and pink throughout. Do not overcook, as the shrimp will continue to cook once removed from the heat.
- Stir in parsley, salt, and pepper to taste.
- Meanwhile, cook linguine according to package instructions. Drain and add to the pan with the shrimp and sauce. Toss to coat.

- Serve immediately with lemon wedges, if desired.

Nutrition per Serving (based on 4 servings):
- Calories: 520
- Fat: 18g
- Saturated Fat: 3g
- Cholesterol: 220mg
- Sodium: 530mg
- Carbohydrates: 64g
- Fiber: 2g
- Sugar: 3g
- Protein: 32g

Tips:
- For a creamier sauce, stir in 1/4 cup of heavy cream or full-fat coconut milk before adding the shrimp.
- Add chopped sun-dried tomatoes or roasted red peppers for extra flavor and texture.
- If you don't have white wine, you can substitute it with chicken broth or water.
- Serve this dish with a side of steamed broccoli or roasted vegetables for a complete and balanced meal.

Slow Cooker Solutions

Beef Chili with Black Beans:

Ingredients:

- 1 tablespoon olive oil
- 1 pound lean ground beef (90% lean or higher)
- 1 onion, chopped
- 2 cloves garlic, minced
- 1 red bell pepper, chopped
- 1 green bell pepper, chopped
- 1 jalapeño pepper, seeded and chopped (optional)
- 1 (28-ounce) can crushed tomatoes, undrained
- 1 (15-ounce) can black beans, rinsed and drained
- 1 (14.5-ounce) can diced tomatoes, undrained
- 1 (15-ounce) can kidney beans, rinsed and drained
- 1 cup beef broth
- 2 tablespoons chili powder
- 1 tablespoon cumin
- 1 teaspoon smoked paprika
- 1/2 teaspoon dried oregano
- 1/4 teaspoon cayenne pepper (optional)
- Salt and freshly ground black pepper, to taste

Instructions:

- Heat olive oil in a large Dutch oven or pot over medium heat. Add ground beef and cook until browned, breaking it up with a spoon. Drain off any excess fat.
- Add onion, garlic, bell peppers, and jalapeño (if using) to the pot. Cook until softened, about 5 minutes.
- Stir in crushed tomatoes, black beans, diced tomatoes, kidney beans, beef broth, chili powder, cumin, paprika, oregano, and cayenne pepper (if using). Season with salt and pepper to taste.
- Bring to a boil, then reduce heat to low and simmer for at least 30 minutes, or longer for thicker chili. Stir occasionally.
- Taste and adjust seasonings as needed. Serve hot with your favorite toppings, such as shredded cheese, sour cream, chopped onions, avocado, or cilantro.

Nutrition per Serving (based on 6 servings):

- Calories: 400
- Fat: 16 grams
- Saturated fat: 6 grams
- Cholesterol: 90 milligrams
- Sodium: 650 milligrams
- Carbohydrates: 42 grams
- Fiber: 15 grams
- Sugar: 8 grams
- Protein: 30 grams

Tips:

- To make this chili even heartier, you can add other vegetables, such as corn, carrots, or zucchini.
- You can also use ground turkey or chicken instead of ground beef.
- Leftovers can be stored in an airtight container in the refrigerator for up to 3 days.

Moroccan Chicken Tagine:

Ingredients (serves 4-6):
- 2 tablespoons olive oil
- 1 large onion, chopped
- 2 cloves garlic, minced
- 1 teaspoon ground ginger
- 1/2 teaspoon turmeric
- 1/4 teaspoon ground cinnamon
- 1/4 teaspoon ground coriander
- 1/4 teaspoon cayenne pepper (optional, adjust to your spice preference)
- 1/2 teaspoon salt
- 1/4 teaspoon black pepper
- 1 pound bone-in, skin-on chicken thighs
- 1 (14.5 oz) can diced tomatoes, undrained
- 1/2 cup chicken broth
- 1/4 cup dried apricots
- 1/4 cup slivered almonds
- 1 tablespoon honey
- Chopped fresh cilantro, for garnish (optional)
- Couscous, for serving (optional)

Instructions:
- Heat olive oil in a large Dutch oven or tagine over medium heat. Add onion and cook until softened, about 5 minutes. Stir in garlic, ginger, turmeric, cinnamon, coriander, cayenne pepper (if using), salt, and black pepper. Cook for 1 minute, until fragrant.
- Add chicken thighs and brown on all sides, about 5 minutes per side.
- Pour in diced tomatoes and chicken broth. Stir in apricots and bring to a simmer. Cover and cook for 20-25 minutes, or until chicken is cooked through.
- Stir in honey and almonds. Reduce heat to low and simmer for 5 more minutes, allowing the flavors to meld.
- Garnish with chopped cilantro (optional) and serve with fluffy couscous.

Nutrition per serving (estimated):
- Calories: 450-500
- Protein: 40-45 grams
- Fat: 20-25 grams
- Carbohydrates: 40-45 grams
- Fiber: 5-6 grams
- Sugar: 10-15 grams

Tips:
- You can use boneless, skinless chicken thighs for a shorter cooking time, but the bone-in, skin-on thighs add more flavor.
- Feel free to adjust the spices to your taste preference.
- For a vegetarian option, replace the chicken with chickpeas or tofu.
- Serve with roasted vegetables or a side salad for a complete meal.

Creamy White Bean Stew (Slow Cooker or Stovetop):

Ingredients:
- 1 tablespoon olive oil
- 1 onion, chopped
- 2 carrots, chopped
- 2 celery stalks, chopped

- 2 cloves garlic, minced
- 1 teaspoon dried thyme
- 1/2 teaspoon dried rosemary
- 1/4 teaspoon red pepper flakes (optional)
- 4 cups vegetable broth
- 1 (15 oz) can cannellini beans, drained and rinsed
- 1 (15 oz) can great northern beans, drained and rinsed
- 1 (14.5 oz) can diced tomatoes, undrained
- 1 cup water
- 1/2 cup heavy cream (can substitute with unsweetened almond milk for a lighter option)
- 1/4 cup chopped fresh parsley
- Salt and black pepper to taste

Instructions (Slow Cooker):
- Heat olive oil in a large skillet over medium heat. Add onion, carrots, and celery, and sauté for 5-7 minutes, until softened.
- Add garlic, thyme, rosemary, and red pepper flakes (if using), and cook for another minute, until fragrant.
- Transfer the vegetable mixture to your slow cooker. Add vegetable broth, beans, diced tomatoes with their juices, and water. Stir to combine.
- Cook on low for 6-8 hours, or on high for 3-4 hours, until the vegetables are tender and the beans are heated through.
- About 30 minutes before serving, stir in heavy cream (or almond milk) and parsley. Season with salt and pepper to taste.

- Serve hot, with crusty bread for dipping, if desired.

Instructions (Stovetop):
- Follow steps 1 and 2 from the slow cooker instructions.
- Transfer the vegetable mixture to a large Dutch oven or pot. Add vegetable broth, beans, diced tomatoes with their juices, and water. Stir to combine.
- Bring to a boil, then reduce heat and simmer for 20-25 minutes, or until the vegetables are tender and the beans are heated through.
- Follow steps 5 and 6 from the slow cooker instructions.
- Serve hot, with crusty bread for dipping, if desired.

Nutrition per Serving (based on 6 servings):
- Calories: 320
- Fat: 13g
- Saturated Fat: 3g
- Cholesterol: 30mg
- Sodium: 340mg
- Carbohydrates: 42g
- Fiber: 10g
- Sugar: 7g
- Protein: 17g

Tips:
- For a thicker stew, mash some of the beans with a fork before adding the heavy cream.
- You can substitute cannellini beans and great northern beans with other white beans like chickpeas or navy beans.

- Add chopped kale or spinach for extra greens.
- If you prefer a vegan version, substitute the heavy cream with unsweetened almond milk or coconut milk and garnish with a sprinkle of nutritional yeast for a cheesy flavor.

Wraps & Bowls

Hummus Veggie Wraps:

Ingredients (for 4 wraps):
- 4 whole-wheat tortillas
- 1/2 cup hummus (choose your favorite flavor!)
- 1/2 cup sliced baby spinach
- 1/2 cup shredded carrots
- 1/2 cup cucumber slices
- 1/4 cup crumbled feta cheese (optional)
- 1/4 cup sliced red onion (optional)
- Drizzle of olive oil (optional)

Instructions:
- Spread hummus evenly on each tortilla.
- Layer your favorite vegetables on top of the hummus. Get creative! Some additional ideas include sliced bell peppers, tomatoes, avocado, sprouts, or grilled chicken.
- Sprinkle on feta cheese and red onion, if using.
- Drizzle with olive oil, if desired.
- Roll up the tortillas tightly and enjoy!

Nutrition Facts per Serving:
- Calories: 280
- Fat: 10g (healthy fats from hummus and olive oil)
- Carbohydrates: 35g (complex carbs from whole-wheat tortillas)
- Fiber: 8g (excellent for digestive health)
- Protein: 10g (keeps you feeling full and energized)
- Sodium: 300mg (watch your intake if on a restricted sodium diet)

Tips:
- Make a big batch of hummus on the weekend to have it readily available for wraps throughout the week.
- Choose seasonal vegetables for the freshest flavor and nutrients.
- Add a kick of protein with grilled chicken or tofu.
- Get creative with the toppings! Experiment with different herbs, spices, and sauces.

Buddha Bowl with Quinoa & Tahini Dressing:

Ingredients:
For the Quinoa:
- ¾ cup quinoa, rinsed
- 1 ½ cups water
- Pinch of salt

For the Roasted Vegetables:
- 1 ½ cups broccoli florets
- 1 ½ cups cauliflower florets
- 1 red bell pepper, chopped
- 1 tablespoon olive oil
- ½ teaspoon dried oregano
- ½ teaspoon smoked paprika
- Pinch of salt and black pepper

For the Tahini Dressing:
- ¼ cup tahini paste
- 2 tablespoons lemon juice

- 2 tablespoons water
- 1 tablespoon maple syrup
- 1 clove garlic, minced
- ¼ cup chopped fresh parsley
- Pinch of salt and black pepper

For the Bowl:
- ½ cup cooked lentils (optional)
- ½ avocado, sliced
- ¼ cup cherry tomatoes, halved
- ¼ cup crumbled feta cheese
- Handful of fresh spinach or kale

Instructions:
- Cook the quinoa: Rinse the quinoa and add it to a saucepan with the water and salt. Bring to a boil, then reduce heat, cover, and simmer for 15 minutes, or until all the water is absorbed. Fluff with a fork and set aside.
- Roast the vegetables: Preheat the oven to 400°F (200°C). Toss the broccoli, cauliflower, and bell pepper with olive oil, oregano, paprika, salt, and pepper. Spread on a baking sheet and roast for 20-25 minutes, or until tender and slightly browned.
- Make the tahini dressing: In a blender or food processor, combine the tahini, lemon juice, water, maple syrup, garlic, parsley, salt, and pepper. Blend until smooth and creamy. Taste and adjust seasonings if needed.

Chicken Caesar Salad Wraps:

Ingredients (for 4 wraps):
- 1 boneless, skinless chicken breast (approximately 6 oz)
- 1 tablespoon olive oil

- Assemble the bowl: Divide the cooked quinoa, lentils (if using), roasted vegetables, avocado slices, cherry tomatoes, and feta cheese among individual bowls. Drizzle each bowl with tahini dressing, top with fresh spinach or kale, and enjoy!

Nutrition per serving (based on one bowl):
- Calories: 450
- Carbohydrates: 50g (19g fiber)
- Protein: 18g
- Fat: 18g (3g saturated)
- Dietary Fiber: 19g
- Vitamin A: 20% Daily Value
- Vitamin C: 40% Daily Value
- Iron: 20% Daily Value
- Calcium: 10% Daily Value

Tips:
- Feel free to customize this recipe with your favorite vegetables, protein sources, and toppings.
- Leftovers can be stored in an airtight container in the refrigerator for up to 3 days.
- For a vegan option, omit the feta cheese and use a vegan-friendly tahini paste.
- Make a big batch of the tahini dressing and store it in the refrigerator for easy lunches throughout the week.

- Salt and pepper to taste
- 4 large romaine lettuce leaves
- 1/2 cup shredded cooked chicken

- 1/4 cup Caesar dressing (choose a lighter variety if desired)
- 1/4 cup grated Parmesan cheese
- 1/4 cup cherry tomatoes, halved (optional)

Instructions:
- Preheat the oven to 400°F (200°C).
- Place the chicken breast in a baking dish and drizzle with olive oil. Season with salt and pepper.
- Bake for 15-20 minutes, or until the chicken is cooked through and juices run clear.
- Let the chicken cool slightly, then shred it with two forks.
- Wash and dry the romaine lettuce leaves.
- Spread a thin layer of Caesar dressing on each lettuce leaf.
- Top with shredded chicken, Parmesan cheese, and cherry tomatoes (if using).
- Roll up the lettuce leaves tightly, enclosing the filling.
- Enjoy immediately!

Nutrition per serving (approximate):
- Calories: 300
- Fat: 10 grams
- Carbohydrates: 15 grams
- Protein: 30 grams
- Fiber: 2 grams
- Sodium: 400 mg (depending on your choice of dressing)

Tips:
- You can grill or pan-fry the chicken instead of baking it.
- Add other vegetables like chopped avocado, cucumbers, or red onion for extra flavor and nutrients.
- Use whole-wheat tortillas instead of romaine lettuce for a heartier wrap.
- Make the wraps ahead of time and store them in the refrigerator for up to 24 hours.

Light & Refreshing

Caprese Salad with Grilled Halloumi:

Ingredients (for 2 servings):
- 1 ripe tomato, sliced
- 1 ball (8 oz) halloumi cheese, cut into 1/2-inch thick slices
- 1/2 cup baby spinach or arugula
- 1/4 cup basil leaves, roughly torn
- 1 tablespoon olive oil
- 1 tablespoon balsamic vinegar
- Salt and black pepper to taste

Instructions:
- Heat a grill pan or skillet over medium heat. Brush the halloumi slices with olive oil.
- Grill the halloumi for 2-3 minutes per side, or until golden brown and slightly softened.
- While the halloumi is grilling, arrange the tomato slices on a plate or shallow bowl. Top with the baby spinach or arugula and basil leaves.
- Once the halloumi is cooked, place it on top of the salad. Drizzle with olive oil and balsamic vinegar.
- Season with salt and black pepper to taste and serve immediately.

Nutrition per serving (approximate):
- Calories: 340
- Fat: 20 g (saturated 10 g)
- Carbohydrates: 24 g (fiber 4 g, sugar 14 g)
- Protein: 18 g
- Sodium: 360 mg

Tips:
- For a vegetarian option, omit the halloumi and add chickpeas or cooked lentils for additional protein.
- Use different types of tomatoes for a variety of colors and flavors.
- Add a drizzle of pesto for a burst of flavor.
- Serve with crusty bread for dipping.

Mediterranean Couscous Salad:

Ingredients:
- 1 cup pearl couscous
- 1 1/2 cups vegetable broth
- 1 tablespoon olive oil
- 1/2 small red onion, finely chopped
- 1 clove garlic, minced
- 1/2 cup grape tomatoes, halved
- 1/2 cucumber, chopped
- 1/4 cup kalamata olives, pitted and halved
- 1/4 cup crumbled feta cheese
- 1/4 cup chopped fresh parsley
- 2 tablespoons lemon juice
- 1 tablespoon olive oil
- Salt and pepper to taste

Instructions:
- In a medium saucepan, heat the vegetable broth and olive oil to a boil. Remove from heat and stir in the couscous. Cover and let stand for 10 minutes, or until the couscous is fluffy and all the liquid has been

absorbed. Fluff the couscous with a fork.

- While the couscous is cooking, sauté the red onion in a separate pan with a little olive oil until softened. Add the garlic and cook for another minute until fragrant.
- In a large bowl, combine the cooled couscous, sautéed onions and garlic, tomatoes, cucumber, olives, feta cheese, and parsley.
- In a small bowl, whisk together the lemon juice, olive oil, salt, and pepper to make the dressing.
- Pour the dressing over the salad and toss to combine.
- Serve at room temperature or chilled.

Nutrition per Serving (based on 6 servings):
- Calories: 290
- Fat: 12 grams (1.5 grams saturated)
- Carbohydrates: 41 grams (4 grams fiber)
- Protein: 10 grams
- Sodium: 320 mg

Tips:
- Feel free to customize this recipe with your favorite Mediterranean ingredients. Add bell peppers, artichoke hearts, grilled chicken, or chickpeas for even more protein and flavor.
- Make this salad ahead of time for a quick and easy lunch option. It will keep in the refrigerator for up to 3 days.
- Use whole-wheat couscous for a boost of fiber and nutrients.
- Adjust the amount of lemon juice and olive oil in the dressing to your taste.

Warm & Comforting:

Chicken Pot Pie Soup:

Ingredients (Serves 4):
- 1 tablespoon olive oil
- 1 medium onion, chopped
- 2 celery stalks, chopped
- 2 carrots, chopped
- 4 cloves garlic, minced
- 1/2 teaspoon dried thyme
- 1/4 teaspoon dried rosemary
- 1/2 teaspoon salt
- 1/4 teaspoon black pepper
- 4 cups chicken broth
- 2 cups cooked chicken, shredded or diced
- 1 cup frozen peas
- 1 cup frozen corn
- 1 cup potatoes, peeled and diced (cubed sweet potato adds a nice twist)
- 1/2 cup milk (light cream or unsweetened almond milk can be used)
- 1/4 cup all-purpose flour
- 1/4 cup chopped fresh parsley (optional)

Instructions:
- Heat olive oil in a large pot or Dutch oven over medium heat. Add onion, celery, and carrots, and cook until softened, about 5 minutes. Stir in garlic, thyme, rosemary, salt, and pepper. Cook for another minute until fragrant.
- Pour in the chicken broth and bring to a boil. Reduce heat and simmer for 5 minutes.
- Add cooked chicken, peas, corn, and potatoes. Simmer for another 5 minutes, or until potatoes are tender.
- In a small bowl, whisk together milk and flour until smooth. Slowly whisk the milk mixture into the soup, stirring constantly until it thickens slightly. Simmer for an additional minute.
- Garnish with chopped parsley (optional) and serve hot with crusty bread or crackers.

Nutrition per Serving (Approximate):
- Calories: 350
- Fat: 15g
- Carbohydrates: 40g
- Fiber: 5g
- Protein: 30g
- Sodium: 800mg (adjust according to broth used)

Tips:
- This soup can be made with leftover chicken or rotisserie chicken for added convenience.
- Don't have milk? You can substitute a little extra broth or a plant-based milk like unsweetened almond milk.
- Feel free to add other vegetables like green beans, mushrooms, or broccoli.
- For a thicker soup, mash some of the potatoes before adding them to the broth.

- If you prefer a dairy-free option, omit the milk and flour, and thicken the soup with cornstarch instead.

Lentil Shepherd's Pie:

Ingredients:
For the lentil filling:
- 1 tablespoon olive oil
- 1/2 onion, chopped
- 1 carrot, chopped
- 2 celery stalks, chopped
- 2 cloves garlic, minced
- 1 cup green lentils, rinsed
- 4 cups vegetable broth
- 1 can (14.5 oz) diced tomatoes, undrained
- 1 teaspoon dried thyme
- 1/2 teaspoon dried rosemary
- Salt and pepper to taste

For the mashed potato topping:
- 4 medium potatoes, peeled and chopped
- 1/2 cup milk (dairy or plant-based)
- 2 tablespoons butter or vegan butter
- Salt and pepper to taste

Instructions:
- Preheat the oven to 400°F (200°C).
- Heat olive oil in a large ovenproof pot or Dutch oven over medium heat. Add the onion, carrot, and celery, and cook until softened, about 5 minutes.
- Add the garlic and cook for 30 seconds until fragrant.
- Stir in the lentils, broth, tomatoes, thyme, and rosemary. Season with salt and pepper to taste. Bring to a boil, then reduce heat and simmer for 20 minutes, or until the lentils are tender and the sauce has thickened.
-
- While the lentils are simmering, cook the potatoes in a pot of boiling water until tender, about 15 minutes. Drain and return them to the pot.
- Mash the potatoes with the milk and butter or vegan butter, until smooth and creamy. Season with salt and pepper to taste.
- Spoon the lentil mixture into a baking dish. Top with the mashed potato topping, making sure to spread it evenly.
- Bake for 20-25 minutes, or until the potato topping is golden brown and bubbly.
- Let cool for 5 minutes before serving.

Nutrition per Serving (assuming 6 servings):
- Calories: 380
- Fat: 15g (saturated 4g)
- Carbs: 50g (fiber 7g)
- Protein: 18g
- Sodium: 350mg
- Cholesterol: 0mg

Tips:
- You can use brown lentils for a slightly earthy flavor.

- Add other vegetables to the filling, such as diced mushrooms, bell peppers, or zucchini.

- For a richer flavor, add a tablespoon of tomato paste to the lentil mixture.
- Make this dish ahead of time and reheat it in the oven before serving.

Global Flavors at Home:

Thai Shrimp Curry:

Ingredients (Serves 4):

- 1 tablespoon vegetable oil
- 1 red bell pepper, sliced
- 1 green bell pepper, sliced
- 1 onion, chopped
- 2 cloves garlic, minced
- 1 tablespoon grated ginger
- 1 tablespoon red curry paste (adjust to your spice preference)
- 1 can (14 oz) unsweetened coconut milk
- 1 cup vegetable broth
- 1 tablespoon brown sugar
- 1 pound raw shrimp, peeled and deveined
- 1/2 cup chopped fresh cilantro
- Lime wedges, for serving
- Cooked rice, for serving (optional)

Instructions:

- Heat oil in a large skillet or Dutch oven over medium heat. Add the bell peppers and onion, and cook until softened, about 5 minutes.
- Stir in the garlic and ginger, and cook for 30 seconds, until fragrant.
- Add the red curry paste and cook until fragrant, about 1 minute.
- Pour in the coconut milk and vegetable broth, and stir in the brown sugar. Bring to a simmer.
- Add the shrimp and cook for 2-3 minutes, or until opaque and cooked through.
- Remove from heat and stir in the cilantro.
- Serve immediately with lime wedges and cooked rice, if desired.

Nutrition per Serving (approximate):

- Calories: 420
- Fat: 18g
- Saturated Fat: 5g
- Carbohydrates: 45g
- Fiber: 5g
- Sugar: 14g
- Protein: 32g
- Sodium: 580mg

Tips:

- Feel free to substitute other vegetables, such as broccoli, zucchini, or carrots.
- Add a can of drained and rinsed bamboo shoots for a more traditional Thai curry flavor.
- Use full-fat coconut milk for a richer flavor, but keep in mind the increased calorie and fat content.
- Serve with fresh basil or Thai basil instead of cilantro, if desired.
- Make it spicier by adding a pinch of red pepper flakes or sriracha.

Italian Meatballs with Zucchini Noodles:

Ingredients:

Meatballs:

- 1/2 pound ground beef (90% lean)
- 1/2 pound ground pork
- 1/2 cup breadcrumbs
- 1/4 cup grated Parmesan cheese
- 1/4 cup chopped fresh parsley
- 1 large egg, beaten
- 1 clove garlic, minced
- 1/2 teaspoon onion powder
- 1/2 teaspoon dried oregano
- 1/4 teaspoon salt
- 1/4 teaspoon black pepper

Sauce:

- 1 tablespoon olive oil
- 1/2 onion, chopped
- 2 cloves garlic, minced
- 1 (28-ounce) can crushed tomatoes
- 1/2 teaspoon dried basil
- 1/4 teaspoon dried oregano
- Pinch of red pepper flakes (optional)
- Salt and pepper to taste

Noodles:

- 2 medium zucchini
- 1 tablespoon olive oil
- Salt and pepper to taste

Instructions:

- Make the meatballs: In a large bowl, combine the ground beef, pork, breadcrumbs, Parmesan cheese, parsley, egg, garlic, onion powder, oregano, salt, and pepper. Mix well until evenly combined.
- Form the meatballs: Roll the mixture into 12 equal-sized meatballs.
- Heat the olive oil: In a large skillet over medium heat, heat the olive oil.
- Brown the meatballs: Add the meatballs to the skillet and cook until browned on all sides, about 5-7 minutes.
- Transfer the meatballs: Carefully remove the browned meatballs from the skillet and set them aside on a plate.
- Sauté the onions and garlic: In the same skillet, add the chopped onion and sauté until softened, about 3 minutes. Add the minced garlic and cook for another minute.
- Add the tomatoes and herbs: Add the crushed tomatoes, basil, oregano, and red pepper flakes (if using) to the skillet. Season with salt and pepper to taste.
- Simmer the sauce: Bring the sauce to a simmer, then add the browned meatballs back to the skillet. Reduce heat to low and simmer for 20-25 minutes, or until the meatballs are cooked through and the sauce has thickened.
- Make the zucchini noodles: While the sauce simmers, spiralize the zucchini into noodles using a spiralizer or vegetable peeler.
- Cook the noodles: Heat the olive oil in a separate skillet over medium heat. Add the zucchini noodles and cook for 2-3 minutes, stirring occasionally, until slightly softened. Season with salt and pepper to taste.
- Serve: Divide the zucchini noodles between two plates and top with the meatballs and sauce. Enjoy hot!

Nutrition per serving (based on 2 servings):

- Calories: 550
- Fat: 26 g
- Carbohydrates: 43 g

- Fiber: 8 g
- Protein: 42 g
- Sodium: 650 mg

Tips:
- You can use all ground beef or all ground pork if you prefer.
- Add other vegetables to the sauce, such as chopped carrots, bell peppers, or mushrooms.
- To make vegetarian meatballs, substitute the ground meat with lentil or black bean crumbles.
- Serve the meatballs and sauce over whole-wheat pasta or rice instead of zucchini noodles for a different option.

Korean Bibimbap Bowls:

Ingredients (for 4 servings):

For the rice:
- 2 cups water
- 1 1/2 cups long-grain white rice
- 1 teaspoon toasted sesame oil
- 1/2 teaspoon salt

For the vegetables:
- 1 small carrot, julienned
- 1/2 cucumber, julienned
- 1 cup spinach, trimmed and chopped
- 4 shiitake mushrooms, thinly sliced (optional)
- 1/2 cup bean sprouts
- 1 tablespoon sesame oil
- 1 teaspoon soy sauce
- 1/2 teaspoon sesame seeds

For the meat:
- 1/2 pound ground beef or ground turkey
- 1 tablespoon soy sauce
- 1 teaspoon sesame oil
- 1/2 teaspoon ginger, minced
- 1/4 teaspoon garlic, minced
- Pinch of black pepper

For the egg:
- 1 egg
- 1 tablespoon vegetable oil

For the sauce:
- 2 tablespoons gochujang (Korean chili paste)
- 1 tablespoon soy sauce
- 1 tablespoon honey
- 1 tablespoon rice vinegar
- 1 teaspoon sesame oil
- 1/2 teaspoon garlic, minced

Instructions:
- Cook the rice: Rinse the rice and combine it with water, sesame oil, and salt in a rice cooker or pot. Cook according to package instructions or until fluffy and cooked through.
- Prepare the vegetables: Julienne the carrot and cucumber. Blanch the spinach in boiling water for 30 seconds, then drain and squeeze out excess water. If using, slice the shiitake mushrooms. In a separate bowl, toss the bean sprouts with sesame oil, soy sauce, and sesame seeds. Set aside.
- Cook the meat: Heat a pan over medium heat. Add the ground beef or turkey and cook until browned, breaking it up with a spatula. Drain any excess fat. Stir in the soy sauce,

sesame oil, ginger, garlic, and black pepper. Cook for an additional minute until fragrant.

- Fry the egg: Heat the vegetable oil in a small pan over medium heat. Crack the egg into the pan and fry until sunny-side up.
- Assemble the bowls: Divide the cooked rice equally among four bowls. Top each bowl with the prepared vegetables, cooked meat, and a fried egg. Drizzle with the prepared sauce and enjoy!

Nutrition per serving (approximate):
- Calories: 450
- Fat: 15g
- Carbohydrates: 55g
- Protein: 25g
- Fiber: 5g
- Sodium: 600mg

Tips:
- You can adjust the vegetables used in this recipe based on your preferences. Other options include shredded zucchini, broccoli florets, or pickled radishes.
- Feel free to customize the spiciness of the sauce to your liking. Add more gochujang for a spicier bibimbap, or less for a milder version.
- For a vegetarian option, omit the meat and tofu cubes or other plant-based protein.
- This recipe is easily doubled or tripled to feed a crowd.

Falafel Pita Pockets:

Ingredients (yields 4-6 pita pockets):
For the falafel:
- 1 can (15 oz) chickpeas, drained and rinsed
- 1/2 cup fresh parsley, chopped
- 1/4 cup fresh cilantro, chopped
- 1/4 cup red onion, finely chopped
- 2 cloves garlic, minced
- 1/2 teaspoon ground cumin
- 1/2 teaspoon coriander powder
- 1/4 teaspoon paprika
- 1/4 teaspoon cayenne pepper (optional)
- 1/4 cup bread crumbs or oat flour
- Salt and pepper to taste
- Vegetable oil for frying or baking

For the toppings:
- 4-6 whole wheat pita breads
- 1/2 cup hummus
- 1/2 cup chopped tomatoes
- 1/2 cup chopped cucumber
- 1/4 cup chopped red onion (optional)
- 1/4 cup tahini sauce (optional)
- Fresh parsley, chopped, for garnish
- Lemon wedges, for serving

Instructions:
- Make the falafel: In a food processor, combine chickpeas, parsley, cilantro, red onion, garlic, cumin, coriander, paprika, cayenne pepper (if using), bread crumbs or oat flour, salt, and pepper. Pulse until a coarse mixture forms. Do not over-process, it should still be slightly chunky.

- Form the falafel balls: Wet your hands and shape the mixture into small balls, about the size of a ping-pong ball. If it's too wet, add a little more bread crumbs or oat flour.
- Fry or bake the falafel: Heat vegetable oil in a large skillet over medium heat. Fry the falafel balls for 3-4 minutes per side, until golden brown and crispy. Alternatively, you can bake them on a baking sheet preheated to 400°F for 12-15 minutes, flipping halfway through.
- Assemble the pita pockets: Warm the pita breads in a pan or microwave for about 30 seconds. Spread hummus on the inside of each pita bread. Top with falafel balls, chopped tomatoes, cucumber, red onion (if using), tahini sauce (if using), and parsley.
- Serve: Enjoy your falafel pita pockets warm, with lemon wedges on the side for a refreshing squeeze.

Nutrition per serving (approximate):
- Calories: 400-450
- Fat: 15-20g
- Carbohydrates: 40-45g
- Fiber: 8-10g
- Protein: 15-20g
- Sodium: 300-400mg

Tips:
- Make the falafel mixture ahead of time and store it in the refrigerator for up to 2 days.
- You can also use pre-made falafel if you're short on time.
- Add other toppings to your liking, such as lettuce, spinach, olives, or feta cheese.
- Try different types of hummus for a variety of flavors.

Family-Friendly & Flavorful Dinner Ideas for Every Night:

Quick & Easy Weeknight Delights:

One-Pan Chicken Fajitas:

Ingredients (serves 4):

- 1 pound boneless, skinless chicken breasts, thinly sliced
- 1 bell pepper, sliced (color of your choice)
- 1 red onion, sliced
- 2 cloves garlic, minced
- 1 tablespoon fajita seasoning (or a combination of chili powder, cumin, paprika, garlic powder, and onion powder)
- 1 tablespoon vegetable oil
- 1/4 cup water or chicken broth
- 4 large tortillas (whole wheat or corn)
- Toppings of your choice: chopped avocado, salsa, guacamole, sour cream, shredded cheese, cilantro, lime wedges

Instructions:

- Preheat the oven to 400°F (200°C).
- In a large bowl, toss chicken, bell pepper, onion, garlic, fajita seasoning, and oil until well coated.
- Spread the mixture evenly on a rimmed baking sheet.
- Pour water or broth around the edges of the pan.
- Bake for 20-25 minutes, or until chicken is cooked through and vegetables are tender-crisp.
- While the chicken is cooking, warm your tortillas according to package instructions.
- Assemble your fajitas: Fill each tortilla with chicken, vegetables, and your desired toppings.
- Serve immediately with lime wedges on the side.

Nutrition per serving (approximate):

- Calories: 400-450
- Fat: 15-20g
- Carbohydrates: 35-40g
- Fiber: 3-5g
- Protein: 30-35g
- Sodium: 350-400mg

Tips:

- You can use any type of bell pepper you like, or even a mix of colors for a more vibrant dish.
- For a spicier kick, add a few dashes of hot sauce or chopped jalapeños to the fajita seasoning.
- Shrimp or tofu can be substituted for the chicken for a vegetarian option.
- Leftovers can be stored in an airtight container in the refrigerator for up to 3 days.

Creamy Tomato Pasta with Spinach:

Ingredients (serves 4):
- 1 tablespoon olive oil
- 1/2 onion, finely chopped
- 2 cloves garlic, minced
- 1 (28 oz) can crushed tomatoes
- 1/2 cup chicken broth or vegetable broth
- 1/2 cup heavy cream (can substitute with unsweetened almond milk or light cream for a lighter option)
- 1/4 teaspoon dried oregano
- 1/4 teaspoon dried basil
- Salt and pepper to taste
- 8 ounces pasta (penne, rigatoni, or your favorite shape)
- 4-5 ounces baby spinach
- Freshly grated Parmesan cheese, for serving

Instructions:
- Heat the olive oil in a large skillet over medium heat. Add the onion and cook until softened, about 5 minutes.
- Stir in the garlic and cook for 30 seconds until fragrant.
- Add the crushed tomatoes, chicken broth, heavy cream, oregano, basil, salt, and pepper. Bring to a simmer and cook for 5 minutes, stirring occasionally.
- Meanwhile, cook the pasta according to package instructions. Drain and set aside.
- Stir the spinach into the tomato sauce until wilted, about 1 minute.
- Add the cooked pasta to the sauce and toss to combine.
- Serve immediately with freshly grated Parmesan cheese.

Nutrition per serving (approximate):
- Calories: 450-500
- Fat: 15-20g
- Carbohydrates: 50-55g
- Fiber: 5-6g
- Protein: 15-20g
- Sodium: 400-500mg

Tips:
- Use any type of pasta you like. Whole-wheat pasta will increase the fiber content.
- For a richer flavor, you can add a tablespoon of tomato paste to the sauce.
- Add a pinch of red pepper flakes if you like it spicy.
- You can also add other vegetables to the sauce, such as chopped bell peppers, mushrooms, or zucchini.
- This dish is delicious leftover! Store it in an airtight container in the refrigerator for up to 3 days

Salmon with Lemon & Broccoli:

Ingredients (serves 4):
- 4 salmon filets (4-6 oz each)
- 1 tablespoon olive oil
- 1/2 teaspoon salt
- 1/4 teaspoon black pepper
- 1 large head broccoli, cut into florets

- 1 lemon, thinly sliced
- 2 tablespoons butter, softened
- 1/4 cup fresh parsley, chopped (optional)

Instructions:

- Preheat the oven to 400°F (200°C). Line a baking sheet with parchment paper.
- Place the salmon filets on the prepared baking sheet. Drizzle with olive oil and season with salt and pepper.
- Arrange the broccoli florets around the salmon. Tuck the lemon slices between the broccoli and salmon filets.
- Dot the salmon with softened butter.
- Bake for 15-20 minutes, or until the salmon is cooked through and the broccoli is tender-crisp.
- Garnish with chopped parsley (optional) and serve immediately.

Nutrition per serving (approximate):

- Calories: 450-500
- Fat: 25-30g
- Carbohydrates: 15-20g
- Fiber: 4-5g
- Protein: 40-45g
- Sodium: 400-500mg

Tips:

- For thicker lemon sauce, whisk the pan juices with 1 tablespoon of cornstarch before serving.
- Substitute asparagus, green beans, or Brussels sprouts for broccoli for a different flavor profile.
- Top with grilled or roasted vegetables for a more substantial meal.
- Add fresh herbs like dill or thyme for additional flavor.
- You can also broil the salmon for a few minutes at the end for a crispier crust

Turkey Burgers with Sweet Potato Fries:

Ingredients:

For the turkey burgers (makes 4-6 burgers):

- 1 pound ground turkey (90% lean)
- 1/2 cup red onion, finely chopped
- 1/4 cup fresh parsley, chopped
- 1/4 cup panko breadcrumbs
- 1 tablespoon Dijon mustard
- 1 teaspoon Worcestershire sauce
- 1/2 teaspoon garlic powder
- 1/2 teaspoon smoked paprika
- 1/4 teaspoon salt
- 1/4 teaspoon black pepper
- Vegetable oil for cooking

For the sweet potato fries:

- 2 large sweet potatoes, peeled and cut into thick wedges
- 1 tablespoon olive oil
- 1/2 teaspoon paprika
- 1/4 teaspoon garlic powder
- 1/4 teaspoon salt
- 1/4 teaspoon black pepper

Instructions:

For the turkey burgers:

- In a large bowl, combine ground turkey, red onion, parsley, breadcrumbs, Dijon mustard, Worcestershire sauce, garlic powder, paprika, salt, and pepper. Mix gently until just combined.
- Divide the mixture into 4-6 equal portions and shape into patties. Make a slight indentation in the center of each patty with your thumb to prevent bulging during cooking.
- Heat a grill pan or skillet over medium heat with a thin layer of oil. Grill the turkey burgers for 3-4 minutes per side, or until cooked through.

For the sweet potato fries:
- Preheat the oven to 425°F (220°C). Line a baking sheet with parchment paper.
- In a large bowl, toss sweet potato wedges with olive oil, paprika, garlic powder, salt, and pepper. Arrange in a single layer on the prepared baking sheet.
- Roast for 20-25 minutes, or until tender and golden brown, flipping halfway through.

Assemble and serve:
- Build your turkey burgers on hamburger buns with your favorite toppings. Enjoy alongside the crispy sweet potato fries!

Nutrition per serving (approximate):
- Turkey burger: 300-350 calories, 25-30g protein, 15-20g carbs, 10-15g fat
- Sweet potato fries (per serving): 150-200 calories, 4-5g protein, 30-35g carbs, 5-10g fat

Tips:
- Add other ingredients to your turkey burger mixture, such as grated cheese, chopped vegetables, or chopped nuts.
- Serve the turkey burgers with a side salad for a more complete meal.
- Dip your sweet potato fries in ketchup, sriracha mayo, or your favorite dipping sauce.
- For a lighter option, bake the turkey burgers instead of grilling.

Pizza Night Done Right: Two Delicious and Customizable Options

Option 1: Classic Margherita Pizza

Ingredients (makes 2 medium pizzas):
Pizza dough:
- 1 1/2 teaspoons active dry yeast
- 1 teaspoon sugar
- 1 1/4 cups warm water (105°F)
- 1 1/2 teaspoons olive oil
- 3 1/2 cups all-purpose flour
- 1 1/2 teaspoons salt

Toppings:
- 2 tablespoons olive oil
- 1 clove garlic, minced
- 1 (28-ounce) can crushed tomatoes
- 1 teaspoon dried oregano
- 1/2 teaspoon salt
- 1/4 teaspoon pepper

- 8 ounces mozzarella cheese, thinly sliced
- Fresh basil leaves, for garnish
- Optional toppings: Sliced pepperoni, ham, mushrooms, peppers, onions, olives, pineapple

Instructions:

- Make the dough: In a large bowl, combine yeast, sugar, and warm water. Let sit for 5 minutes, until foamy. Stir in olive oil.
- Add flour and salt to the yeast mixture. Mix until a shaggy dough forms. Turn onto a lightly floured surface and knead for 8-10 minutes, until smooth and elastic.
- Place dough in a lightly oiled bowl, cover with plastic wrap, and let rise in a warm place for 1 hour, or until doubled in size.
- Preheat the oven to 450°F (230°C).
- Divide dough in half and roll each half into a 12-inch circle on a lightly floured surface. Transfer to pizza stones or lightly oiled baking sheets.
- Make the sauce: In a small saucepan, heat olive oil over medium heat. Add garlic and cook for 30 seconds, until fragrant. Stir in crushed tomatoes, oregano, salt, and pepper. Bring to a simmer and cook for 5 minutes.
- Spread sauce evenly over each pizza dough, leaving a 1-inch border around the edge. Top with mozzarella cheese and any desired additional toppings.
- Bake for 12-15 minutes, or until the crust is golden brown and cheese is bubbly.

- Garnish with fresh basil leaves and serve immediately.

Nutrition per serving (approximate):
- Calories: 500-550
- Fat: 20-25g
- Carbohydrates: 60-65g
- Fiber: 4-5g
- Protein: 20-25g
- Sodium: 500-600 mg

Option 2: Veggie Delight Pizza

Ingredients (makes 2 medium pizzas)
Pizza dough:
- Same as Option 1

Toppings:
- 2 tablespoons olive oil
- 1 red onion, thinly sliced
- 1 green bell pepper, thinly sliced
- 1 yellow bell pepper, thinly sliced
- 1 zucchini, thinly sliced
- 1/2 cup cherry tomatoes, halved
- 4 ounces goat cheese, crumbled
- 1/4 cup fresh arugula, for garnish
- Balsamic glaze, for drizzling

Instructions:
- Follow steps 1-3 from Option 1 to make the dough.
- Preheat the oven to 450°F (230°C).
- Divide dough in half and roll each half into a 12-inch circle on a lightly floured surface. Transfer to pizza stones or lightly oiled baking sheets.
- Drizzle each pizza dough with olive oil. Arrange onion, bell peppers, and zucchini evenly on top. Sprinkle with cherry tomatoes.

- Bake for 15-20 minutes, or until the crust is golden brown and vegetables are tender-crisp.
- Remove pizzas from the oven and top with goat cheese. Return to the oven for 1-2 minutes, just until the cheese is melted.
- Garnish with arugula and drizzle with balsamic glaze before serving.

Nutrition per serving (approximate):
- Calories: 450-500
- Fat: 15-20g
- Carbohydrates: 55-60g
- Fiber: 5-6g
- Protein: 15-20g
- Sodium: 300-400

Slow Cooker Solutions for Busy Days:

Honey Garlic Chicken & Veggies:

Ingredients (serves 4):
- 1 pound boneless, skinless chicken breasts or thighs, cut into 1-inch pieces
- 1 tablespoon olive oil
- 1/2 teaspoon salt
- 1/4 teaspoon black pepper
- 2 cloves garlic, minced
- 1 tablespoon honey
- 2 tablespoons soy sauce
- 1 tablespoon rice vinegar
- 1 teaspoon cornstarch
- 1 tablespoon minced fresh ginger (optional)
- 1 (15-ounce) can diced tomatoes, undrained
- 1 red bell pepper, sliced
- 1 broccoli head, cut into florets
- 1/2 cup chopped green onions, for garnish (optional)
- Sesame seeds, for garnish (optional)

Instructions:
- Preheat the oven to 400°F (200°C). Line a large baking sheet with parchment paper.
- In a medium bowl, toss chicken with olive oil, salt, and pepper. Arrange in a single layer on the prepared baking sheet.
- In a small bowl, whisk together garlic, honey, soy sauce, rice vinegar, cornstarch, and ginger (if using). Pour the sauce over the chicken.
- Add diced tomatoes, bell pepper, and broccoli florets to the baking sheet. Toss everything to coat evenly with the sauce.
- Bake for 20-25 minutes, or until chicken is cooked through and vegetables are tender-crisp.
- Garnish with chopped green onions and sesame seeds, if desired. Serve immediately with rice or your favorite side.

Tips:
- You can use chicken thighs for a richer flavor, but they will take a few minutes longer to cook.
- Feel free to add other vegetables to the pan, such as carrots, onions, or asparagus.
- For a thicker sauce, mix 1 tablespoon cornstarch with 2 tablespoons water and stir into the sauce after the chicken has cooked.
- Leftovers can be stored in an airtight container in the refrigerator for up to 3 days. Reheat in the oven or microwave.

Pulled Pork Tacos:

Ingredients (makes 6-8 servings):
For the pulled pork:

- 4-5 lb bone-in pork shoulder roast, trimmed of excess fat
- 2 tablespoons olive oil

- 1 tablespoon chili powder
- 1 tablespoon cumin
- 1 teaspoon smoked paprika
- 1/2 teaspoon garlic powder
- 1/2 teaspoon onion powder
- 1/4 teaspoon cayenne pepper (optional)
- 1/2 cup apple cider vinegar
- 1/2 cup chicken broth
- 1/4 cup brown sugar
- 1 tablespoon Worcestershire sauce
- Salt and pepper to taste

For the tacos:
- 8 small corn tortillas
- 1 cup shredded cabbage
- 1/2 cup diced red onion
- 1/4 cup chopped fresh cilantro
- Lime wedges, for serving
- Optional toppings: avocado slices, salsa, cheese, sour cream, pickled onions

Instructions:
- Preheat your slow cooker to low.
- In a small bowl, combine olive oil, chili powder, cumin, paprika, garlic powder, onion powder, and cayenne pepper (if using). Rub the spice mixture liberally all over the pork shoulder.
- Place the pork shoulder in the slow cooker and pour in the apple cider vinegar, chicken broth, brown sugar, and Worcestershire sauce. Season with salt and pepper to taste.
- Cover the slow cooker and cook on low for 8-10 hours, or until the pork is very tender and falling apart easily.

- Remove the pork from the slow cooker and transfer to a large bowl. Using two forks, shred the pork, discarding any large pieces of fat.
- Skim off any excess fat from the cooking liquid in the slow cooker. If desired, you can thicken the sauce by simmering it over medium heat for a few minutes.
- Warm the tortillas in a dry skillet or microwave until softened.
- To assemble the tacos, fill each tortilla with shredded pork, top with cabbage, red onion, cilantro, and a squeeze of lime juice. Drizzle with sauce (if desired) and add any other optional toppings you like.
- Serve immediately and enjoy the flavorful fiesta!

Nutrition per serving (approximate):
- Calories: 450-500
- Fat: 20-25g
- Carbohydrates: 40-45g
- Fiber: 3-4g
- Protein: 35-40g
- Sodium: 500-600 mg

Tips:
- Leftover pulled pork can be stored in the refrigerator for up to 3 days or frozen for up to 3 months.
- Feel free to adjust the spices to your liking.
- Experiment with different types of tortillas, such as flour tortillas or whole wheat tortillas.
- Get creative with your toppings! The possibilities are endless

Lentil & Vegetable Soup:

Ingredients (serves 4-6):

- 1 tablespoon olive oil
- 1 onion, chopped
- 2 carrots, chopped
- 2 celery stalks, chopped
- 2 cloves garlic, minced
- 1 teaspoon dried thyme
- 1/2 teaspoon ground cumin
- 1/4 teaspoon ground coriander
- 1 cup green lentils, rinsed
- 4 cups vegetable broth
- 28-ounce can crushed tomatoes
- 1 cup chopped zucchini
- 1/2 cup chopped kale or spinach
- Salt and pepper to taste
- Optional toppings: Chopped fresh parsley, lemon wedges, crusty bread

Instructions:

- Heat olive oil in a large pot over medium heat. Add onion, carrots, and celery, and cook for 5-7 minutes, until softened. Stir in garlic, thyme, cumin, and coriander, and cook for 30 seconds, until fragrant.
- Add lentils, vegetable broth, crushed tomatoes, and zucchini. Bring to a boil, then reduce heat and simmer for 20-25 minutes, or until lentils are tender.

Beef Chili:

Ingredients:

- 1 tablespoon olive oil
- 1 large onion, diced
- 2 cloves garlic, minced
- 1 green bell pepper, diced
- 1 red bell pepper, diced
- 1 jalapeño pepper, seeded and finely chopped (optional, for extra heat)

- Stir in kale or spinach and cook for 1-2 minutes, until wilted. Season with salt and pepper to taste.
- Serve hot, garnished with chopped parsley, lemon wedges, and crusty bread (optional).

Nutrition per serving (approximate):

- Calories: 300-350
- Fat: 5-6g
- Carbohydrates: 45-50g
- Fiber: 10-12g
- Protein: 15-20g
- Sodium: 400-500mg

Tips:

- Add other vegetables, such as green beans, corn, or mushrooms.
- Use brown lentils for a slightly nuttier flavor and extra fiber.
- Make it heartier by adding cooked brown rice or quinoa.
- For a thicker soup, mash some of the cooked lentils against the side of the pot before adding the kale or spinach.
- Leftovers can be stored in an airtight container in the refrigerator for up to 3 days.

- 1 pound ground beef (90% lean preferred)
- 1 (28-ounce) can crushed tomatoes
- 1 (15-ounce) can kidney beans, drained and rinsed
- 1 (15-ounce) can black beans, drained and rinsed

- 1 (15-ounce) can pinto beans, drained and rinsed
- 1 (14.5-ounce) can diced tomatoes, undrained
- 1 cup beef broth
- 2 tablespoons chili powder
- 1 tablespoon ground cumin
- 1 teaspoon smoked paprika
- 1/2 teaspoon dried oregano
- 1/4 teaspoon cayenne pepper (optional, for extra heat)
- Salt and freshly ground black pepper, to taste
- Toppings (optional): Chopped red onion, shredded cheddar cheese, sour cream, cilantro, avocado slices

Instructions:
- Heat olive oil in a large Dutch oven or pot over medium heat. Add the onion and cook until softened, about 5 minutes. Stir in the garlic and cook for 30 seconds, until fragrant.
- Add the bell peppers and jalapeño (if using) and cook for another 5 minutes, until softened.
- Crumble the ground beef into the pot and cook, breaking it up with a spoon, until browned. Drain any excess fat.
- Stir in the crushed tomatoes, kidney beans, black beans, pinto beans, diced tomatoes, beef broth, chili powder, cumin, paprika, oregano, and cayenne pepper (if using). Season with salt and pepper to taste.
- Bring the chili to a simmer, then reduce heat to low and cook for at least 30 minutes, stirring occasionally, to allow the flavors to meld.
- Taste the chili and adjust seasonings as needed.
- Serve hot with desired toppings, such as chopped red onion, shredded cheddar cheese, sour cream, cilantro, and avocado slices.

Nutrition per serving (approximate):
- Calories: 450-500
- Fat: 15-20g
- Carbohydrates: 45-50g
- Fiber: 10-12g
- Protein: 30-35g
- Sodium: 700-800 mg

Tips:
- This chili can be made ahead of time and stored in the refrigerator for up to 3 days. It will even taste better the next day as the flavors develop further.
- For a thicker chili, mash some of the beans with a fork before adding them to the pot.
- You can substitute ground turkey or chicken for ground beef, or use a combination of meats.
- Serve the chili with cornbread, crusty bread, or crackers for dipping

Chicken Curry with Coconut Milk:

Ingredients (serves 4-6):

- 1 tablespoon vegetable oil
- 1 pound boneless, skinless chicken thighs, cut into bite-sized pieces
- 1 onion, chopped
- 2 cloves garlic, minced
- 1 inch fresh ginger, grated
- 1 red bell pepper, thinly sliced (optional)
- 1 green bell pepper, thinly sliced (optional)
- 1-2 tablespoons red curry paste (adjust to your spice preference)
- 1 (14-ounce) can unsweetened coconut milk
- 1 cup chicken broth
- 1 tablespoon brown sugar
- 1 tablespoon fish sauce
- 1/2 lime, juiced
- 1 cup chopped fresh cilantro
- Cooked rice, for serving
- Optional garnishes: Chopped peanuts, sliced red chili peppers, lime wedges

Instructions:

- Heat oil in a large pot or Dutch oven over medium heat. Add chicken pieces and cook, stirring occasionally, until browned on all sides.
- Add onion, garlic, and ginger. Cook for 2-3 minutes, until softened and fragrant.
- Stir in red bell pepper (if using) and cook for another minute until slightly softened.
- Add red curry paste and cook for 1 minute, stirring constantly to avoid burning.
- Pour in coconut milk and chicken broth. Bring to a simmer and cook for 10 minutes, or until chicken is cooked through.
- Stir in brown sugar, fish sauce, and lime juice. Taste and adjust seasonings as needed.
- Serve hot over cooked rice, garnished with chopped cilantro and your optional toppings.

Nutrition per serving (approximate):

- Calories: 450-500
- Fat: 20-25g
- Carbohydrates: 45-50g
- Fiber: 4-5g
- Protein: 30-35g
- Sodium: 500-600 mg

Tips:

- You can substitute chicken breasts for thighs, but cook them for a shorter time as they cook faster.
- Feel free to add other vegetables to the curry, such as broccoli, carrots, or green beans.
- If you don't have red curry paste, you can use yellow curry paste, but the flavor profile will be slightly different.
- Serve with naan bread, roti, or flatbreads for scooping up the delicious sauce.
- Make it vegetarian by replacing the chicken with chickpeas or tofu.

Global Flavors at Home:

Stir-Fried Chicken & Veggies:

Ingredients (serves 2-3):
Marinade:

- 1 tablespoon soy sauce
- 1 tablespoon rice vinegar
- 1/2 teaspoon sesame oil
- 1 teaspoon minced ginger
- 1/2 teaspoon garlic powder
- 1/4 teaspoon black pepper

For the stir-fry:

- 1 pound boneless, skinless chicken breast, thinly sliced
- 1 tablespoon vegetable oil
- 2 cups of assorted vegetables (broccoli, bell peppers, carrots, sugar snap peas, etc.)
- 1/2 cup chicken broth
- 1 tablespoon cornstarch
- 1/4 cup soy sauce
- 1 tablespoon rice vinegar
- 1 teaspoon honey (optional)
- 1/2 teaspoon sriracha (optional)
- 1/4 cup chopped green onions
- Cooked rice, noodles, or quinoa, for serving

Instructions:

- Marinate the chicken: In a bowl, combine soy sauce, rice vinegar, sesame oil, ginger, garlic powder, and black pepper. Add the chicken slices and toss to coat evenly. Marinate for at least 15 minutes, or up to 30 minutes.
- Prepare the vegetables: Wash and chop your chosen vegetables into bite-sized pieces.

- Cook the chicken: Heat oil in a large wok or skillet over medium-high heat. Add the chicken and cook for 3-4 minutes, or until browned and cooked through. Remove from the pan and set aside.
- Stir-fry the vegetables: Add the prepared vegetables to the pan and stir-fry for 2-3 minutes, or until tender-crisp.
- Make the sauce: In a small bowl, whisk together chicken broth, cornstarch, soy sauce, rice vinegar, honey (if using), and sriracha (if using).
- Combine and finish the stir-fry: Pour the sauce into the pan with the vegetables and simmer for 30 seconds, until thickened. Add the cooked chicken back to the pan and toss to coat with the sauce.
- Serve: Garnish with chopped green onions and serve hot over cooked rice, noodles, or quinoa.

Nutrition per serving (approximate):

- Calories: 400-500
- Fat: 15-20g
- Carbohydrates: 35-40g
- Fiber: 4-5g
- Protein: 30-35g
- Sodium: 500-600 mg (depending on soy sauce content)

Tips:
- Feel free to experiment with different protein sources like tofu, shrimp, or beef.
- Add more vegetables for extra nutrients and fiber.
- For a thicker sauce, add a cornstarch slurry (1 tablespoon cornstarch mixed with 2 tablespoons water) towards the end of cooking.
- Adjust the spice level to your preference.
- Make it a complete meal by serving with a side of brown rice or quinoa.

Taco Tuesday with a Twist: Three Flavorful Variations to Spice Up Your Night!

Option 1: Korean Beef Bulgogi Tacos:

Ingredients (makes 10 tacos):
For the bulgogi marinade:
- 1/4 cup soy sauce
- 2 tablespoons brown sugar
- 2 tablespoons rice vinegar
- 1 tablespoon sesame oil
- 1 tablespoon minced garlic
- 1 tablespoon grated ginger
- 1/2 teaspoon ground black pepper

For the tacos:
- 1 pound skirt steak or flank steak, thinly sliced
- 10 small corn tortillas
- 1 cup shredded cabbage
- 1/2 cup chopped carrots
- 1/4 cup sliced green onions
- Kimchi, sesame seeds, and cilantro, for topping (optional)

Instructions:
- Combine all marinade ingredients in a bowl. Add the sliced steak and marinate for at least 30 minutes, or up to overnight for extra flavor.
- Heat a grill pan or large skillet over medium-high heat. Cook the marinated steak for 2-3 minutes per side, or until desired doneness.
- Warm the tortillas according to package instructions.
- Assemble tacos by filling each tortilla with bulgogi beef, shredded cabbage, carrots, green onions, and your desired toppings. Enjoy!

Nutrition per serving (approximate):
- Calories: 350-400
- Fat: 15-20g
- Carbohydrates: 30-35g
- Fiber: 3-4g
- Protein: 30-35g
- Sodium: 600-700mg (depending on soy sauce)

Option 2: Caribbean Jerk Chicken Tacos:

Ingredients (makes 10 tacos):
For the jerk marinade:
- 1 tablespoon jerk seasoning
- 1/4 cup brown sugar
- 2 tablespoons olive oil
- 2 tablespoons lime juice
- 1 teaspoon soy sauce
- 1/2 teaspoon minced garlic
- 1/4 teaspoon allspice

For the tacos:
- 1 pound boneless, skinless chicken thighs, thinly sliced
- 10 small flour tortillas
- 1 mango, diced
- 1 avocado, diced
- Red onion, sliced
- Cilantro, for garnish

Instructions:
- Combine all marinade ingredients in a bowl. Add the sliced chicken and marinate for at least 2 hours, or up to overnight for maximum flavor.
- Heat a grill pan or large skillet over medium-high heat. Cook the marinated chicken for 2-3 minutes per side, or until cooked through.
- Warm the tortillas according to package instructions.
- Assemble tacos by filling each tortilla with jerk chicken, diced mango, avocado, red onion, and cilantro. Squeeze some fresh lime juice for an extra zesty touch.

Nutrition per serving (approximate):
- Calories: 400-450
- Fat: 20-25g
- Carbohydrates: 40-45g
- Fiber: 4-5g
- Protein: 30-35g
- Sodium: 400-500mg

Option 3: Vegetarian Black Bean and Sweet Potato Tacos:

Ingredients (makes 10 tacos):

For the black bean filling:
- 1 (15 oz) can black beans, drained and rinsed
- 1 tablespoon olive oil
- 1/2 cup chopped onion
- 1/2 cup chopped red bell pepper
- 1/4 cup chopped cilantro
- 1 teaspoon ground cumin
- 1/2 teaspoon chili powder
- 1/4 teaspoon smoked paprika
- Salt and pepper to taste

For the tacos:
- 10 small whole wheat tortillas
- 1 sweet potato, roasted and diced
- 1 avocado, sliced
- Jalapeños, sliced (optional)
- Cilantro lime crema or salsa, for topping

Instructions:
- Heat olive oil in a skillet over medium heat. Add onion and bell pepper, and cook until softened.
- Add black beans, cumin, chili powder, paprika, salt, and pepper. Stir to combine and cook for 5 minutes.Continue to stir and mash some of the beans for a slightly chunky texture.
- Warm the tortillas according to package instructions.
- Assemble tacos by filling each tortilla with black bean mixture, roasted sweet potato, avocado slices, jalapeños (if using), and a dollop of cilantro lime crema or salsa. Enjoy your vegetarian fiesta!

Nutrition per serving (approximate):
- Calories: 300-350

- Fat: 10-15g
- Carbohydrates: 45-50g
- Fiber: 7-8g
- Protein: 15-20g
- Sodium: 400-500mg

No matter which twist you choose, these Taco Tuesday variations promise an explosion of flavor and fun. Experiment with different toppings, salsas, and sides to personalize your fiesta!

Bonus Tip: Leftover fillings can be repurposed for salads, bowls, or wraps, extending the Taco Tuesday magic throughout the week.

Have a delicious and exciting Taco Tuesday! Don't forget to tell me which option you tried and what you loved most in the review section!

Pasta Primavera with Spring Veggies: A Burst of Freshness for Your Palette

Ingredients (serves 4-6):
- 12 ounces pasta (penne, farfalle, or fusilli work well)
- 1 tablespoon olive oil
- 1 small onion, chopped
- 2 cloves garlic, minced
- 1 bunch asparagus, trimmed and cut into 1-inch pieces
- 1 zucchini, sliced
- 1 cup snap peas
- 1/2 cup cherry tomatoes, halved
- 1/4 cup chopped fresh parsley
- 1/4 cup chopped fresh basil
- 1/4 cup grated Parmesan cheese
- Salt and freshly ground black pepper to taste
- Lemon wedge, for serving (optional)

Instructions:
- Cook the pasta: Bring a large pot of salted water to a boil. Add the pasta and cook according to package instructions until al dente (slightly firm to the bite). Drain and set aside.
- Sauté the vegetables: While the pasta cooks, heat olive oil in a large skillet over medium heat. Add the onion and garlic, and cook until softened, about 5 minutes.
- Add the asparagus and zucchini, and cook for another 5 minutes, or until slightly tender-crisp.
- Stir in the snap peas and cherry tomatoes, cook for 1-2 minutes until warmed through.
- Drain any excess liquid from the vegetables if needed.
- Combine and serve: Add the cooked pasta and reserved cooking water (about 1/4 cup) to the skillet with the vegetables. Toss to combine, then stir in the chopped parsley, basil, and Parmesan cheese. Season with salt and pepper to taste.
- Serve immediately with a lemon wedge for a squeeze of zesty freshness, if desired.

Nutrition per serving (approximate):
- Calories: 450-500
- Fat: 15-20g
- Carbohydrates: 60-65g
- Fiber: 5-6g
- Protein: 15-20g
- Sodium: 400-500mg

Tips:
- Feel free to customize this recipe with your favorite spring vegetables!

Broccoli, artichoke hearts, and peashoots are all great additions.
- You can add a protein twist by including grilled chicken, shrimp, or tofu.
- If you like a creamy sauce, add a splash of heavy cream or crème fraîche to the skillet at the end.
- For a vegan option, substitute nutritional yeast for Parmesan cheese and use plant-based butter or olive oil.

Mediterranean Salmon with Lemon & Herbs:

Ingredients (serves 4):
- 4 salmon filets (5-6 oz each)
- 1/4 cup olive oil
- 1/2 lemon, juiced and zested
- 2 cloves garlic, minced
- 1/2 teaspoon dried oregano
- 1/4 teaspoon dried thyme
- Salt and freshly ground black pepper, to taste
- 1/4 cup chopped fresh parsley
- 1/4 cup cherry tomatoes, halved (optional)
- Kalamata olives, sliced (optional)
- Feta cheese, crumbled (optional)

Instructions:
- Preheat the oven to 400°F (200°C). Line a baking sheet with parchment paper.
- Pat the salmon filets dry with paper towels. Season both sides with salt and pepper.
- In a small bowl, whisk together olive oil, lemon juice, lemon zest, garlic, oregano, and thyme. Brush the salmon generously with the sauce on both sides.
- Arrange the salmon filets on the prepared baking sheet. Drizzle any remaining sauce over the top.
- Bake for 12-15 minutes, or until the salmon is cooked through and flakes easily with a fork.
- While the salmon is cooking, prepare the optional toppings. Chop parsley, halve cherry tomatoes, slice Kalamata olives, and crumble feta cheese.
- To serve, plate the salmon with a spoonful of the pan sauce. Garnish with chopped parsley, cherry tomatoes, olives, and feta cheese (if using).

Nutrition per serving (approximate):
- Calories: 450-500
- Fat: 25-30g
- Carbohydrates: 5-10g
- Fiber: 1-2g
- Protein: 40-45g

- Sodium: 400-500mg (depending on sodium content of feta cheese and olives)

Tips:

- For extra flavor, marinate the salmon in the lemon-herb sauce for 30 minutes before baking.

- Substitute cod or pollock for salmon if desired.
- Serve with roasted vegetables like zucchini, bell peppers, or asparagus for a complete meal.
- Add a side of couscous or quinoa for a grain-based option.
- Drizzle with additional lemon juice before serving for a bright finishing touch.

Sheet Pan Fajita Bowls:

Ingredients (makes 4-6 servings):
For the fajitas:

- 1 pound boneless, skinless chicken breasts, thinly sliced
- 1 bell pepper (red, yellow, or orange), thinly sliced
- 1 red onion, thinly sliced
- 1 tablespoon olive oil
- 1 tablespoon lime juice
- 1 teaspoon chili powder
- 1/2 teaspoon cumin
- 1/2 teaspoon smoked paprika
- 1/4 teaspoon garlic powder
- 1/4 teaspoon salt
- 1/4 teaspoon black pepper

For the bowls:

- 4-6 cups cooked brown rice or quinoa
- Black beans, pinto beans, or chickpeas, drained and rinsed (optional)
- Guacamole or salsa
- Shredded cheese (cheddar, Monterey Jack, or cotija)
- Chopped fresh cilantro
- Sliced avocado (optional)
- Tortillas (optional)

Instructions:

- Preheat the oven to 425°F (220°C).
- In a large bowl, combine chicken slices with olive oil, lime juice, chili powder, cumin, paprika, garlic powder, salt, and pepper. Toss to coat evenly.
- Add bell pepper and onion slices to the bowl and mix well. Spread the mixture onto a large baking sheet in a single layer.
- Roast for 20-25 minutes, or until chicken is cooked through and vegetables are tender-crisp.
- While the fajitas roast, cook your chosen grain (brown rice, quinoa, etc.) according to package instructions.
- Divide cooked grain into bowls and top with the roasted fajita mixture. Add your desired toppings: black beans, guacamole or salsa, cheese, cilantro, avocado slices, and tortillas (if using).

Nutrition per serving (approximate):

- Calories: 500-600
- Fat: 20-25g

- Carbohydrates: 50-60g
- Fiber: 8-10g
- Protein: 30-35g
- Sodium: 400-500mg (depending on added salt and toppings)

Tips:

- For a vegetarian option, replace the chicken with tofu cubes or crumbled tempeh, marinated in the same spices.
- Add other vegetables to the sheet pan, like zucchini, mushrooms, or poblano peppers.
- Season the guacamole or salsa with additional lime juice and chopped cilantro for an extra burst of flavor.
- Use pre-cooked black beans or canned Chipotle black beans for added smoky depth.
- Get creative with toppings! Experiment with chopped lettuce, corn, sour cream, olives, or your favorite hot sauce.

Weekend Feasts & Potlucks:

Lasagna Roll-Ups:

Ingredients (makes 12-15 roll-ups):

For the meat sauce:

- 1 tablespoon olive oil
- 1 pound ground beef or Italian sausage
- 1/2 onion, chopped
- 2 cloves garlic, minced
- 1 (28-ounce) can crushed tomatoes
- 1/2 cup dry red wine (optional)
- 1 teaspoon dried oregano
- 1/2 teaspoon dried basil
- Salt and pepper to taste

For the ricotta filling:

- 15 ounces whole-milk ricotta cheese
- 1/2 cup grated Parmesan cheese
- 1/4 cup chopped fresh parsley
- 1 large egg
- Salt and pepper to taste

For the assembly:

- 12 lasagna noodles, cooked according to package instructions
- 1 (15 ounces) container ricotta cheese
- 1 1/2 cups shredded mozzarella cheese

Instructions:

- Make the meat sauce: Heat olive oil in a large skillet over medium heat. Add ground beef or sausage and cook until browned, breaking it up with a spoon. Drain any excess fat.
- Add onion and garlic to the skillet and cook until softened, about 5 minutes. Stir in crushed tomatoes, red wine (if using), oregano, basil, salt, and pepper. Bring to a simmer and cook for 15 minutes, stirring occasionally.
- Make the ricotta filling: In a bowl, combine ricotta cheese, Parmesan cheese, parsley, egg, salt, and pepper. Stir until well mixed.
- Assemble the roll-ups: Spread a thin layer of meat sauce on a flat surface. Lay a cooked lasagna noodle on top and spread about 1/4 cup of ricotta filling evenly over the noodle. Tightly roll up the noodle, starting from the short end. Repeat with remaining noodles and filling.
- Preheat the oven to 375°F (190°C). Pour a thin layer of meat sauce into the bottom of a 9x13 inch baking dish. Arrange the lasagna roll-ups, seam side down, in the dish.
- Pour remaining meat sauce over the top of the roll-ups and sprinkle with mozzarella cheese.
- Cover the baking dish with foil and bake for 20 minutes. Remove foil and bake for an additional 10-15 minutes, or until the cheese is melted and bubbly.
- Let cool for 10 minutes before serving. Enjoy!

Nutrition per serving (approximate):

- Calories: 450-500
- Fat: 20-25g
- Carbohydrates: 40-45g
- Fiber: 3-4g
- Protein: 25-30g
- Sodium: 600-700mg (depending on ingredients)

Tips:
- You can substitute ground turkey or chicken for the beef or sausage.
- Add chopped spinach or other vegetables to the ricotta filling for extra nutrients.
- Use pre-made meat sauce to save time.
- For a vegetarian option, replace the meat sauce with a marinara sauce or a lentil Bolognese.
- Leftovers can be stored in an airtight container in the refrigerator for up to 3 days.

Chicken Pot Pie:

Ingredients (makes 8-10 servings):
For the filling:
- 1 tbsp olive oil
- 1 pound boneless, skinless chicken breasts, cut into bite-sized pieces
- 1/2 onion, chopped
- 2 carrots, diced
- 2 celery stalks, diced
- 1 clove garlic, minced
- 4 cups chicken broth
- 1/2 cup frozen peas
- 1/4 cup all-purpose flour
- 1/2 cup milk
- 1/4 tsp dried thyme
- Salt and pepper to taste

For the crust:
- 2 cups all-purpose flour
- 1/2 teaspoon salt
- 1/2 cup cold unsalted butter, cubed
- 1/4 cup ice water

Instructions:
- Preheat oven to 400°F (200°C).
- Heat olive oil in a large Dutch oven or oven-safe pot over medium heat. Add chicken and cook until golden brown on all sides.
- Add onion, carrots, and celery, and cook until softened, about 5 minutes. Add garlic and cook for another minute.
- Pour in chicken broth and bring to a boil. Reduce heat, cover, and simmer for 15 minutes, or until chicken is cooked through.
- Stir in frozen peas and cook for 1 minute.
- In a small bowl, whisk together flour and milk until smooth. Slowly whisk into the simmering pot until thickened. Add thyme, salt, and pepper to taste.
- Make the crust: In a large bowl, whisk together flour and salt. Using a pastry cutter or your fingers, blend in the butter until it forms coarse crumbs. Gradually add ice water, a tablespoon at a time, until the dough just comes together. Avoid overmixing.
- On a lightly floured surface, roll out the dough into a circle slightly larger than the top of your pot. Transfer the dough to the pot, trimming any excess. Crimp the edges to seal.

- Brush the crust with milk and cut a few slits for steam to vent.
- Bake for 30-35 minutes, or until the crust is golden brown and the filling is bubbly. Let cool slightly before serving.

Nutrition per serving (approximate):
- Calories: 450-500
- Fat: 20-25g
- Carbohydrates: 40-45g
- Fiber: 3-4g
- Protein: 30-35g

- Sodium: 500-600mg (depending on chicken broth)

Tips:
- Feel free to swap the vegetables for your favorites, like corn, green beans, or mushrooms.
- Add a tablespoon of chopped fresh parsley for extra flavor.
- Use pre-made pie crust to save time, but homemade always adds a special touch.
- Leftovers can be stored in an airtight container in the refrigerator for up to 3 days

Beef & Broccoli Stir-Fry:

Ingredients (serves 4):
For the marinade:
- 1 tablespoon soy sauce
- 1 tablespoon cornstarch
- 1/2 teaspoon sesame oil
- 1/4 teaspoon black pepper

For the stir-fry:
- 1 pound flank steak or sirloin steak, thinly sliced
- 1 tablespoon vegetable oil
- 1 clove garlic, minced
- 1 inch fresh ginger, grated
- 1 head broccoli, cut into florets
- 1 small bell pepper, sliced (optional)
- 1/2 cup low-sodium chicken broth
- 1/4 cup soy sauce
- 1 tablespoon oyster sauce (optional)
- 1 tablespoon brown sugar
- 1 tablespoon cornstarch
- 1/4 cup chopped green onions
- Cooked rice, for serving

Instructions:
- Marinate the beef: In a bowl, combine soy sauce, cornstarch, sesame oil, and black pepper. Add the sliced beef and toss to coat. Marinate for at least 30 minutes, or up to overnight for deeper flavor.
- Prepare the vegetables: Wash and cut the broccoli into florets. Slice the bell pepper (optional).
- Make the sauce: In a small bowl, whisk together chicken broth, soy sauce, oyster sauce (if using), brown sugar, and cornstarch.
- Heat the oil: Heat a large wok or frying pan over high heat. Add vegetable oil and swirl to coat.
- Stir-fry the beef: Add the marinated beef and cook for 2-3 minutes, or until browned and cooked through. Remove from the pan and set aside.

- Stir-fry the vegetables: Add the broccoli and bell pepper (if using) to the pan. Stir-fry for 2-3 minutes, or until crisp-tender.
- Add the sauce: Pour the prepared sauce into the pan with the vegetables. Bring to a simmer and cook for 1 minute, stirring constantly, to thicken.
- Return the beef: Add the cooked beef back to the pan and toss to combine with the sauce and vegetables.
- Finish and serve: Garnish with chopped green onions and serve immediately over cooked rice.

Nutrition per serving (approximate):
- Calories: 450-500
- Fat: 15-20g
- Carbohydrates: 40-45g
- Fiber: 4-5g
- Protein: 30-35g
- Sodium: 800-900mg (depending on soy sauce)

Tips:
- For a vegetarian option, replace the beef with tofu or tempeh, cubed and marinated in the same way.
- Add other vegetables like carrots, snap peas, or water chestnuts for additional variety.
- Feel free to adjust the amount of garlic, ginger, and chili flakes to your spice preference.
- Serve with your favorite stir-fry toppings like chopped peanuts, sesame seeds, or sriracha

Sheet Pan Roasted Chicken & Vegetables:

Ingredients (serves 4):
- 1 1/2 pounds bone-in, skin-on chicken thighs or breasts (thighs will be juicier)
- 1 tablespoon olive oil
- 1/2 teaspoon dried thyme
- 1/2 teaspoon smoked paprika
- 1/2 teaspoon garlic powder
- Salt and freshly ground black pepper, to taste
- 1 red onion, quartered
- 1 bell pepper (your choice of color), sliced
- 1 head broccoli, cut into florets
- 1 cup cherry tomatoes or chopped zucchini (optional)
- 1 tablespoon lemon juice (optional)

Instructions:
- Preheat the oven to 400°F (200°C). Line a large rimmed baking sheet with parchment paper for easy cleanup.
- In a small bowl, combine olive oil, thyme, paprika, garlic powder, salt, and pepper. Pat the chicken dry with paper towels and rub the spice mixture all over the chicken pieces.
- Arrange the chicken thighs or breasts on the prepared baking sheet. Scatter the onion, bell pepper, and broccoli florets around the chicken. If using, add the cherry tomatoes or zucchini at this time.
- Roast for 20-25 minutes for chicken thighs, or 15-20 minutes for chicken breasts, or until the chicken is

cooked through and the vegetables are tender-crisp.
- If desired, drizzle the roasted chicken and vegetables with a tablespoon of lemon juice before serving.

Nutrition per serving (approximate):
- Calories: 450-500
- Fat: 20-25g
- Carbohydrates: 30-35g
- Fiber: 5-6g
- Protein: 35-40g
- Sodium: 500-600mg (depending on added salt)

Tips:

One-Pot Pasta Primavera:

Ingredients (serves 4-6):
- 1 tablespoon olive oil
- 1 red onion, finely chopped
- 3 cloves garlic, minced
- 1/2 teaspoon dried oregano
- 1/2 teaspoon red pepper flakes (optional)
- 4 cups vegetable broth or chicken broth (for vegetarian option)
- 1 (15 oz) can diced tomatoes, undrained
- 1 cup green beans, trimmed and cut into 1-inch pieces
- 1 cup asparagus, trimmed and cut into 1-inch pieces
- 1 zucchini, diced
- 1 cup sun-dried tomatoes, chopped (optional)

- For extra flavor, marinate the chicken in the spice mixture for at least 30 minutes before roasting.
- Don't overcrowd the pan! Make sure the chicken and vegetables have space to roast evenly.
- Add other vegetables to your liking, such as carrots, Brussels sprouts, or green beans.
- For a more flavorful sauce, toss the roasted vegetables with a teaspoon of Dijon mustard or balsamic vinegar before serving.
- This recipe is great for meal prep! Let the chicken and vegetables cool slightly, then store in an airtight container in the refrigerator for up to 3 days. Reheat in the oven or microwave before serving.

- 12 oz short pasta, like penne, fusilli, or orecchiette
- 1/2 cup chopped fresh basil
- 1/4 cup grated Parmesan cheese (optional)
- Salt and freshly ground black pepper to taste

Instructions:
- Heat olive oil in a large Dutch oven or pot over medium heat. Add chopped onion and cook until softened, about 5 minutes.
- Stir in minced garlic, oregano, and red pepper flakes (if using) and cook for another minute until fragrant.
- Pour in the vegetable broth, diced tomatoes, green beans, asparagus,

and zucchini. Bring to a boil, then reduce heat and simmer for 5 minutes, or until vegetables are nearly tender.

- Add sun-dried tomatoes (if using) and uncooked pasta. Stir to combine and cook for 8-10 minutes, or until pasta is al dente and sauce thickens slightly.
- Remove from heat and stir in chopped fresh basil. Season with salt and pepper to taste.
- Serve immediately, topped with grated Parmesan cheese (optional), and enjoy the fresh flavors of spring in every bite!

Nutrition per serving (approximate):

- Calories: 400-450
- Fat: 10-15g
- Carbohydrates: 55-60g
- Fiber: 5-6g
- Protein: 15-20g
- Sodium: 500-600mg (depending on broth)

Tips:

- Feel free to customize this recipe with your favorite spring vegetables! Broccoli, peas, snap peas, or artichoke hearts are all great additions.
- For a richer flavor, use a combination of vegetable broth and chicken broth.

Plant-Based Powerhouses:

Black Bean Burgers: Two Delicious and Customizable Versions

Option 1: Smoky Chipotle Black Bean Burgers:

Ingredients (makes 6 burgers):
- 1 (15 oz) can black beans, drained and rinsed
- 1/2 cup cooked quinoa or brown rice
- 1/4 cup chopped red onion
- 1/4 cup chopped red bell pepper
- 2 cloves garlic, minced
- 1 tablespoon chopped cilantro
- 1 tablespoon chipotle pepper in adobo sauce, finely chopped (adjust to spice preference)
- 1 teaspoon olive oil
- 1/2 cup bread crumbs
- 1/4 cup rolled oats
- 1/2 teaspoon ground cumin
- 1/2 teaspoon smoked paprika
- Salt and pepper to taste
- Hamburger buns, toppings of your choice (lettuce, tomato, avocado, onion, cheese, etc.)

Instructions:
- Preheat oven to 400°F (200°C). Line a baking sheet with parchment paper.
- In a food processor, pulse the black beans until coarsely chopped. Transfer to a large bowl.
- Add cooked quinoa or brown rice, red onion, red bell pepper, garlic, cilantro, chipotle pepper (adjust for spice), olive oil, bread crumbs, oats, cumin, and paprika. Season with salt and pepper to taste.
- Mix well to combine and form into 6 equal patties.
- Place patties on the prepared baking sheet and bake for 15-20 minutes, or until firm and slightly golden brown.
- Assemble burgers on toasted buns with your desired toppings. Enjoy!

Nutrition per serving (approximate):
- Calories: 300-350
- Fat: 10-15g
- Carbohydrates: 35-40g
- Fiber: 8-10g
- Protein: 20-25g
- Sodium: 300-400mg

Option 2: Southwestern Black Bean and Corn Burgers:

Ingredients (makes 6 burgers):
- 1 (15 oz) can black beans, drained and rinsed
- 1/2 cup corn kernels, fresh or frozen
- 1/4 cup chopped red onion
- 1/4 cup chopped green bell pepper
- 2 cloves garlic, minced
- 1/4 cup chopped fresh cilantro
- 1 tablespoon lime juice
- 1/2 teaspoon ground cumin
- 1/2 teaspoon chili powder
- 1/4 cup rolled oats
- 1/4 cup shredded cheddar cheese
- Salt and pepper to taste
- Hamburger buns, toppings of your choice (lettuce, tomato, avocado, onion, salsa, etc.)

Instructions:

- In a food processor, pulse the black beans until coarsely chopped. Transfer to a large bowl.
- Add corn kernels, red onion, green bell pepper, garlic, cilantro, lime juice, cumin, chili powder, oats, and cheddar cheese. Season with salt and pepper to taste.
- Mix well to combine and form into 6 equal patties.
- Heat a grill pan or skillet over medium heat. Lightly coat with oil if desired.
- Cook patties for 3-4 minutes per side, or until golden brown and heated through.
- Assemble burgers on toasted buns with your desired toppings. Enjoy!

Nutrition per serving (approximate):

- Calories: 350-400
- Fat: 15-20g
- Carbohydrates: 30-35g
- Fiber: 5-7g
- Protein: 20-25g
- Sodium: 400-500mg

Tips:

- Adjust the spice levels to your preference.
- Add other ingredients like chopped zucchini, mushrooms, or jalapenos for additional flavor and texture.
- Try different types of beans like pinto beans or kidney beans for variety.
- Serve the burgers with avocado crema, guacamole, or your favorite burger sauce.

Lentil Shepherd's Pie:

Ingredients (serves 4-6):

For the lentil filling:

- 1 tablespoon olive oil
- 1 onion, chopped
- 2 carrots, chopped
- 2 celery stalks, chopped
- 2 cloves garlic, minced
- 1 tablespoon tomato paste
- 1 cup green lentils, rinsed
- 4 cups vegetable broth
- 1 (14.5 oz) can diced tomatoes, undrained
- 1 teaspoon dried thyme
- 1/2 teaspoon dried rosemary
- Salt and pepper to taste

For the mashed potato topping:

- 2 pounds potatoes, peeled and cubed
- 1/2 cup milk (dairy or plant-based)
- 2 tablespoons butter or vegan butter
- Salt and pepper to taste

Instructions:

- Preheat oven to 400°F (200°C).
- Heat olive oil in a large Dutch oven or ovenproof pot over medium heat. Add the onion, carrots, and celery, and cook until softened, about 5 minutes. Stir in the garlic and cook for 1 minute more.
- Add tomato paste and stir to coat the vegetables. Then, add lentils,

vegetable broth, diced tomatoes, thyme, rosemary, salt, and pepper. Bring to a boil, then reduce heat and simmer for 20-25 minutes, or until lentils are tender.

- While the lentils are simmering, boil the potatoes in a separate pot until fork-tender. Drain and return to the pot. Mash with milk, butter, and salt and pepper until smooth.

- Spoon the lentil mixture into an even layer in the Dutch oven. Top with the mashed potatoes, spreading evenly with a fork.

- Bake for 20-25 minutes, or until the potato topping is golden brown and bubbly.

- Let cool for a few minutes before serving. Enjoy hot with a sprinkle of additional fresh herbs if desired.

Nutrition per serving (approximate):

- Calories: 450-500
- Fat: 15-20g
- Carbohydrates: 55-60g
- Fiber: 10-12g
- Protein: 20-25g
- Sodium: 700-800mg (depending on broth)

Tips:

- For a richer flavor, use browned ground beef or lamb instead of lentils. Simply cook the meat in the pot before adding the vegetables.

- Add other vegetables to the filling, such as chopped mushrooms, green beans, or corn.

- You can also use mashed sweet potatoes for the topping for a sweeter flavor and additional vitamin A.

- Leftovers can be stored in an airtight container in the refrigerator for up to 3 days. Reheat in the oven or microwave.

Tofu Scramble with Veggies:

Ingredients (serves 2-3):

For the tofu scramble:
- 14 oz firm or extra-firm tofu, drained and pressed
- 1 tablespoon olive oil
- 1/2 onion, diced
- 1/2 bell pepper, diced
- 2 cloves garlic, minced
- 1/4 cup chopped mushrooms (optional)
- 1/2 teaspoon turmeric powder
- 1/4 teaspoon smoked paprika

- 1/4 teaspoon black pepper
- 1/4 cup vegetable broth
- 1/4 cup nutritional yeast (optional)
- Salt to taste

For the garnish (optional):
- Chopped avocado
- Sliced tomato
- Fresh herbs (cilantro, chives, parsley)
- Hot sauce

91

Instructions:

- Crumble the tofu: Use your hands or a fork to crumble the tofu into small pieces. Aim for a texture similar to scrambled eggs.
- Sauté the vegetables: Heat olive oil in a large skillet over medium heat. Add the onion and bell pepper and cook until softened, about 5 minutes. Add the garlic and mushrooms (if using) and cook for another minute.
- Add spices and tofu: Stir in the turmeric, paprika, and black pepper. Add the crumbled tofu and cook for 3-4 minutes, stirring occasionally, until slightly browned.
- Moisturize and season: Pour in the vegetable broth and scrape up any browned bits from the bottom of the pan. Simmer for a few minutes until the liquid is mostly absorbed. Add nutritional yeast (if using) and salt to taste.

- Serve and enjoy: Transfer the tofu scramble to plates and garnish with your desired toppings. Enjoy warm with toast, tortillas, or a side of fruit.

Nutrition per serving (approximate):

- Calories: 300-350
- Fat: 15-20g
- Carbohydrates: 20-25g
- Fiber: 3-4g
- Protein: 20-25g
- Sodium: 300-400mg (depending on broth)

Tips:

- Feel free to adjust the vegetables to your liking. Spinach, kale, broccoli, and zucchini are all great additions.
- Add a kick of spice with a pinch of red pepper flakes or chili powder.
- For a richer flavor, try using tamari or coconut aminos instead of vegetable broth.

Pasta Primavera with Pesto:

Ingredients (serves 4-6):
For the vegetables:

- 1 tablespoon olive oil
- 1 small red onion, thinly sliced
- 2 cloves garlic, minced
- 1 zucchini, thinly sliced
- 1 yellow bell pepper, thinly sliced
- 1 cup asparagus, trimmed and cut into 1-inch pieces
- 1 cup broccoli florets
- 1/2 cup sugar snap peas (optional)
- 1/2 cup cherry tomatoes, halved

For the pasta and sauce:

- 12 ounces dried pasta (penne, fusilli, or your favorite shape)
- 1/2 cup pesto (homemade or store-bought)
- 1/4 cup grated Parmesan cheese
- 1/4 cup chopped fresh basil (optional)
- Salt and pepper to taste

Instructions:

- Prepare the vegetables: Heat olive oil in a large skillet over medium heat.

Add onion and garlic, and cook until softened, about 3 minutes.

- Add zucchini, bell pepper, asparagus, and broccoli. Cook for 5-7 minutes, stirring occasionally, until vegetables are tender-crisp.
- If using sugar snap peas, add them during the last 2 minutes of cooking.
- Cook the pasta: Meanwhile, cook the pasta according to package instructions until al dente. Reserve about 1/2 cup of the pasta water before draining.
- Combine the pasta and vegetables: In a large bowl, combine cooked pasta, vegetables, pesto, Parmesan cheese, and reserved pasta water. Toss to coat everything evenly.
- Season and garnish: Season with salt and pepper to taste. Garnish with fresh basil (optional) and serve immediately.

Nutrition per serving (approximate):
- Calories: 450-500
- Fat: 15-20g
- Carbohydrates: 55-60g
- Fiber: 5-6g
- Protein: 15-20g
- Sodium: 400-500mg (depending on pesto and Parmesan cheese)

Tips:
- For a creamier sauce, add a splash of heavy cream or full-fat milk to the pesto.
- Add other seasonal vegetables like green beans, peas, or baby corn for even more variety.
- If you don't have fresh basil for garnish, you can use chopped parsley or dill.
- Serve this dish with grilled chicken, shrimp, or tofu for a complete protein-packed meal.

Mushroom & Lentil Bolognese:

Ingredients (serves 4-6):
- 2 tablespoons olive oil
- 1 medium onion, chopped
- 1 carrot, chopped
- 2 stalks celery, chopped
- 2 cloves garlic, minced
- 1 lb mixed mushrooms (cremini, portobello, button, etc.), chopped
- 1/2 cup dry green lentils
- 1 (28-ounce) can crushed tomatoes
- 1 cup vegetable broth
- 1 tablespoon tomato paste
- 1 teaspoon dried oregano
- 1/2 teaspoon dried thyme
- Salt and freshly ground black pepper, to taste
- Fresh parsley, chopped, for garnish (optional)
- Parmesan cheese, grated, for serving (optional)

Instructions:
- Heat olive oil in a large pot or Dutch oven over medium heat. Add onion, carrot, and celery, and cook until softened, about 5 minutes.
- Add garlic and cook for 30 seconds until fragrant.

- Stir in chopped mushrooms and cook for 5-7 minutes, or until browned and softened.
- Add lentils and stir to coat in the oil and vegetables.
- Pour in crushed tomatoes, vegetable broth, tomato paste, oregano, and thyme. Season generously with salt and pepper.
- Bring the mixture to a boil, then reduce the heat to low and simmer for 30-40 minutes, or until the lentils are tender and the sauce has thickened. Be sure to stir occasionally and adjust seasonings as needed.
- Serve the bolognese over your favorite pasta, quinoa, or polenta. Garnish with chopped parsley and Parmesan cheese, if desired.

Nutrition per serving (approximate):
- Calories: 400-450
- Fat: 15-20g
- Carbohydrates: 50-55g
- Fiber: 8-10g
- Protein: 20-25g
- Sodium: 600-700mg (depending on broth and tomato sauce)

Tips:
- For a richer flavor, add a splash of red wine to the pan after adding the garlic.
- You can use pre-cooked lentils to save time, but be sure to adjust the cooking time accordingly.
- Add a pinch of red pepper flakes or a chopped chili pepper for a touch of heat.

Satisfying & Blood Sugar-Friendly Snacks & Sides:

Fresh & Crunchy:

Carrot sticks with hummus or avocado dip:

Ingredients:
For the carrot sticks:
- 2-3 large carrots, peeled and cut into thin sticks (about 3-4 inches long and 1/2 inch thick)

For the Hummus (makes about 1 cup):
- 1 (15 oz) can chickpeas, drained and rinsed
- 1/4 cup tahini
- 2 tablespoons olive oil
- 2 tablespoons lemon juice
- 1 clove garlic, minced
- 1/2 teaspoon salt
- 1/4 cup water (optional)

For the Avocado Dip (makes about 1 cup):
- 1 ripe avocado, peeled and mashed
- 1/4 cup lemon juice
- 1 tablespoon olive oil
- 1/4 teaspoon salt
- 1/4 teaspoon black pepper
- Pinch of red pepper flakes (optional)

Instructions:
- For the carrot sticks: Simply wash and peel the carrots, then cut them into thin sticks.

For the Hummus:
- Combine all ingredients (except water) in a food processor or blender.
- Process until smooth, adding water one tablespoon at a time if needed to reach a desired consistency.
- Taste and adjust seasonings as needed.

For the Avocado Dip:
- Combine all ingredients in a bowl and mash together until smooth.
- Adjust seasonings as needed.

Nutrition per serving (approximate):
- Serving size: 1 cup carrot sticks with 1/4 cup hummus OR 1/4 cup avocado dip

Calories:
- Hummus: 250-300
- Avocado dip: 200-250

Fat:
- Hummus: 15-20g
- Avocado dip: 20-25g

Carbohydrates:
- Hummus: 25-30g
- Avocado dip: 10-15g

Fiber:
- Hummus: 5-7g
- Avocado dip: 4-5g

Protein:
- Hummus: 7-10g
- Avocado dip: 2-3g

Sodium:
- Hummus: 400-500mg
- Avocado dip: 150-200mg

Tips:
- Get creative with your carrot sticks! Try cutting them into different shapes or sizes for variety.
- Add more vegetables to your hummus or avocado dip by blending

in roasted red peppers, spinach, or zucchini.
- Use whole-wheat pita bread or crackers for scooping the dips instead of chips.

- For a spicier kick, add a pinch of cayenne pepper to either dip.
- Hummus and avocado dip can be stored in an airtight container in the refrigerator for up to 3 days.

Apple slices with almond butter:

Ingredients (yields 1 serving):
- 1 medium apple, washed and sliced
- 2 tablespoons almond butter
- Optional toppings: cinnamon, sliced nuts, dried fruit, honey

Instructions:
- Wash and slice your apple into thin wedges or bite-sized pieces.
- Spread 2 tablespoons of almond butter evenly over the apple slices.
- Enjoy as is, or sprinkle with your preferred toppings like cinnamon, chopped nuts, dried fruit, or a drizzle of honey.

Nutrition per serving (approximate):
- Calories: 250-300
- Fat: 15-20g
- Carbohydrates: 25-30g
- Fiber: 5-7g
- Protein: 5-7g

- Sodium: 100-150mg

Tips:
- Choose your favorite apple variety! Different types offer unique flavors and textures.
- For a creamier spread, microwave the almond butter for a few seconds before using.
- Get creative with your toppings! Explore different options, like chia seeds, hemp seeds, or a sprinkle of dark chocolate chips.
- Make this recipe ahead of time for a grab-and-go snack. Place the apple slices and almond butter in a container and enjoy throughout the day.
- This recipe is easily customizable for dietary restrictions. Use nut-free seed butter for nut allergies, or choose a sugar-free almond butter for a lower-sugar option.

Celery sticks with peanut butter and raisins:

Ingredients (per serving):
- 2-3 celery stalks, washed and trimmed,
- 2 tablespoons peanut butter (or alternative nut butter)

- 1/4 cup raisins (golden or dark)

Instructions:

- Spread the peanut butter: Using a butter knife or spoon, spread the peanut butter evenly onto the celery stalks.
- Sprinkle the raisins: Top the peanut butter with a scattering of raisins.

Nutrition per serving (approximate):
- Calories: 150-200
- Fat: 8-10g
- Carbohydrates: 20-25g
- Fiber: 3-4g
- Protein: 5-7g
- Sodium: 150-200mg (depending on peanut butter)

Tips:
- Get creative with your toppings! Try chopped nuts, seeds, sliced bananas, or a drizzle of honey for extra flavor and texture.
- Use almond butter, sunflower seed butter, or another nut/seed butter if you have peanut allergies.
- Make it kid-friendly! Cut the celery into smaller pieces and spread the peanut butter in a thin layer to make it easier for little hands to manage.
- This snack is best enjoyed fresh, but you can store it in an airtight container in the refrigerator for up to 2 days.

Bell pepper slices with cottage cheese:

Ingredients (yields 2-4 servings, depending on pepper size):
- 2 bell peppers (any color you like)
- 1 cup (200g) cottage cheese
- 1/4 cup (25g) chopped fresh herbs (chives, dill, parsley, or a combination)
- 1/4 cup (25g) chopped cucumber (optional)
- 1/4 cup (25g) chopped cherry tomatoes (optional)
- Pinch of salt and pepper to taste
- Fresh cracked black pepper, for garnish (optional)
- Lemon wedges, for serving (optional)

Instructions:

- Wash and dry the bell peppers. Cut them in half lengthwise and remove the seeds and membranes.
- Place the pepper halves on a plate or baking sheet, cut side up.
- In a bowl, combine cottage cheese, chopped herbs, cucumber, and cherry tomatoes (if using). Season with salt and pepper to taste.
- Spoon the cottage cheese mixture into the bell pepper halves, filling them evenly.
- Garnish with fresh cracked black pepper (if using) and serve with lemon wedges (if using).

Nutrition per serving (approximate):
- Calories: 150-200
- Fat: 5-10g

- Carbohydrates: 10-15g
- Fiber: 2-3g
- Protein: 15-20g
- Sodium: 200-300mg (depending on cottage cheese)

Tips:
- Feel free to adjust the amount of herbs and vegetables based on your preferences.
- For a creamier filling, mix in a tablespoon of Greek yogurt with the cottage cheese.

Edamame pods with sea salt:

Ingredients:
- 1 cup frozen edamame pods, shelled
- 1/2 teaspoon sea salt
- Optional: 1/4 teaspoon chili flakes, paprika, garlic powder, or other desired spices

Instructions:
- Bring a pot of water to a boil. Add the edamame pods and cook for 3-5 minutes, depending on their size and desired texture. Drain the water and transfer the edamame to a bowl or plate.
- Sprinkle the sea salt over the edamame. Toss gently to coat evenly.
- (Optional) Add your desired spices. Chili flakes, paprika, garlic powder, or a spice blend of your choice can add a flavor boost. Toss again to combine.
- Serve immediately, and enjoy!

- Add a sprinkle of crumbled feta cheese or chopped olives for extra flavor.
- If you prefer a warm snack, preheat the oven to 350°F (175°C) and bake the stuffed peppers for 10-15 minutes, until slightly heated through.
- This recipe is easily transportable. Pack the stuffed peppers in an airtight container and enjoy them as a mid-day snack at work or school.

Nutrition per serving (approximate):
- Calories: 180-200
- Fat: 8-10g
- Carbohydrates: 15-20g
- Fiber: 3-4g
- Protein: 13-15g
- Sodium: 250-300mg (depending on the amount of sea salt)

Tips:
- For a smoky flavor, roast the edamame pods in the oven for 10-15 minutes on a baking sheet at 400°F (200°C) before adding the spices and salt.
- Use a variety of sea salts, such as black lava salt or pink Himalayan salt, for a different mineral profile.
- Add a squeeze of lemon juice or drizzle of sesame oil for an extra taste dimension.
- Serve with sliced vegetables or mixed greens for a more substantial snack or mini-meal.

Dips & Spreads:

Roasted vegetable crudités with Greek yogurt dip:

Ingredients:

For the roasted vegetables:

- 1 bell pepper (red, yellow, or orange), sliced
- 1 zucchini, sliced
- 1 small red onion, sliced
- 1/2 broccoli head, cut into florets
- 1 tablespoon olive oil
- 1/2 teaspoon dried oregano
- 1/4 teaspoon salt
- 1/4 teaspoon black pepper

For the Greek yogurt dip:

- 1 cup plain Greek yogurt (2%)
- 1/4 cup chopped fresh parsley
- 1/4 cup chopped fresh dill
- 1 tablespoon lemon juice
- 1 clove garlic, minced
- Salt and pepper to taste

Instructions:

- Preheat the oven to 400°F (200°C). Line a baking sheet with parchment paper.
- In a large bowl, toss together the bell pepper slices, zucchini slices, red onion slices, and broccoli florets with olive oil, oregano, salt, and pepper.
- Spread the vegetables on the prepared baking sheet in a single layer.
- Roast for 20-25 minutes, or until tender and slightly browned.
- While the vegetables are roasting, prepare the dip. In a small bowl, combine Greek yogurt, parsley, dill, lemon juice, and garlic. Season with salt and pepper to taste.
- Let the dip chill in the refrigerator for at least 15 minutes to allow the flavors to meld.
- Once the vegetables are done roasting, transfer them to a serving platter. Arrange the crudités around the dip and enjoy!

Nutrition per serving (approximate):

- Calories: 150-200
- Fat: 5-10g
- Carbohydrates: 15-20g
- Fiber: 3-4g
- Protein: 8-10g
- Sodium: 200-300mg

Tips:

- Feel free to add other vegetables to the crudités, such as carrots, cherry tomatoes, or asparagus.
- For a creamier dip, add a few tablespoons of cucumber or avocado to the yogurt mixture.
- Serve the crudités with additional dips, such as hummus or guacamole, for variety.

Homemade guacamole with whole-wheat crackers:

Ingredients: (serves 4-6)

- 2 ripe avocados, halved and pitted
- 1/2 lime, juiced
- 1/4 cup chopped red onion
- 1/4 cup chopped cilantro
- 1 small tomato, seeded and chopped (optional)
- 1 jalapeño pepper, seeded and finely chopped (optional for spice)
- 1/2 teaspoon ground cumin
- 1/4 teaspoon garlic powder
- Salt and freshly ground black pepper, to taste
- Whole-wheat crackers, for serving

Instructions:

- Scoop the flesh of the avocados into a bowl. Mash with a fork or potato masher to your desired consistency, leaving some texture for a chunky guacamole.
- Stir in lime juice, red onion, cilantro, tomato (if using), jalapeño (if using), cumin, and garlic powder.
- Season with salt and pepper to taste. Mix well and adjust seasonings as needed.
- Cover the guacamole with plastic wrap directly touching the surface to prevent browning. Alternatively, drizzle with a little olive oil to create a barrier.
- Refrigerate for at least 30 minutes to allow the flavors to meld, but serve at room temperature.
- Enjoy fresh guacamole with whole-wheat crackers!

Nutrition per serving (approximate):

- Calories: 200-250
- Fat: 15-20g
- Carbohydrates: 15-20g
- Fiber: 5-7g
- Protein: 3-4g
- Sodium: 150-200mg

Tips:

- Choose ripe avocados for the best flavor and texture. They should yield slightly to gentle pressure.
- Adjust the spiciness by adding more or less jalapeño pepper.
- Add other toppings like chopped fresh basil, crumbled feta cheese, or a sprinkle of pumpkin seeds for additional flavor and texture.
- If the guacamole starts to brown, simply stir in a few more drops of lime juice and/or a spoon of fresh salsa.
- Leftover guacamole can be stored in the refrigerator for up to 3 days, but the quality will diminish slightly as it oxidizes.

Black bean salsa with whole-wheat chips:

Ingredients (makes about 2 cups):

- 1 (15 oz) can black beans, drained and rinsed
- 1 cup chopped tomatoes
- 1/2 cup chopped cucumber

- 1/4 cup chopped red onion
- 1/4 cup chopped cilantro
- 1/2 lime, juiced
- 1 tablespoon olive oil
- 1/2 teaspoon chili powder
- 1/4 teaspoon cumin
- Salt and pepper to taste
- Whole-wheat chips, for serving

Instructions:
- In a large bowl, combine black beans, tomatoes, cucumber, red onion, and cilantro.
- Squeeze in the lime juice and drizzle with olive oil.
- Add chili powder, cumin, salt, and pepper. Toss to combine until well coated.
- Taste and adjust seasonings as needed.
- Cover and refrigerate for at least 30 minutes for the flavors to meld.
- Serve chilled with whole-wheat chips for dipping.

Roasted chickpeas with spices:

Ingredients:
- 1 (15-oz) can chickpeas, drained and rinsed
- 1 tablespoon olive oil
- 1/2 teaspoon salt
- 1/4 teaspoon black pepper
- 1/2 teaspoon preferred spice blend (choose from options below or create your own!)
- Optional: Chopped fresh herbs (cilantro, parsley, thyme) for garnish

Spice Blend Options:

Nutrition per serving (approximate):
- Calories: 150-175
- Fat: 5-7g
- Carbohydrates: 20-25g
- Fiber: 4-5g
- Protein: 5-7g
- Sodium: 200-250mg (depending on ingredients)

Tips:
- For a spicier salsa, add a pinch of cayenne pepper or diced jalapeños.
- This salsa is also delicious served over grilled fish or chicken or piled on tacos.
- If you prefer a smoother salsa, you can pulse the ingredients in a food processor until desired consistency is reached.
- Adjust the amount of lime juice and spices to your liking.
- Feel free to add other chopped vegetables like bell peppers, corn, or avocado for even more variety

- Smoky: paprika, cumin, and smoked paprika
- Spicy: chili powder, cayenne pepper, garlic powder
- Indian: curry powder, coriander, turmeric
- Mediterranean: oregano, thyme, garlic powder
- Lemon Herb: rosemary, lemon zest, garlic powder

Instructions:

- Preheat the oven to 400°F (200°C). Line a baking sheet with parchment paper.
- Pat the drained chickpeas dry with a clean kitchen towel to remove excess moisture. This helps them crisp up in the oven.
- In a large bowl, toss the chickpeas with olive oil, salt, pepper, and your chosen spice blend. Make sure the chickpeas are evenly coated.
- Spread the chickpeas in a single layer on the prepared baking sheet.
- Roast for 30-35 minutes, stirring occasionally, until golden brown and crispy. Don't overcrowd the pan, or the chickpeas won't crisp up properly.
- Let the chickpeas cool slightly before serving. Garnish with chopped fresh herbs (optional) and enjoy!

Nutrition per Serving (approximate):

- Calories: 150-175
- Fat: 5-7g
- Carbohydrates: 15-17g
- Fiber: 3-4g
- Protein: 5-7g
- Sodium: 150-200mg (depending on seasoning)

Tips:

- For extra flavor, marinate the chickpeas in your chosen spice blend and olive oil for 30 minutes before roasting.
- Experiment with different spice blends to discover your favorites.
- Roasted chickpeas can be stored in an airtight container at room temperature for up to 3 days.
- Add roasted chickpeas to salads, bowls, or wraps, or enjoy them solo as a satisfying snack.

Hard-boiled eggs with whole-wheat bread:

Ingredients (per serving):

- 2 large eggs
- 2 slices whole-wheat bread
- Optional toppings: Avocado slices, hummus, tomato slices, cucumber slices, sliced cheese, olives, chives, salt, pepper, etc.

Instructions:

- Boil the eggs: Place the eggs in a saucepan and cover with cold water. Bring to a boil, then immediately remove from heat and cover with a lid. Let stand for 12 minutes for perfectly hard-boiled eggs. Alternatively, you can use a steamer or instant pot for quicker cooking times.
- Cool and peel the eggs: Run the eggs under cold water to stop the cooking process and make them easier to peel. Gently tap the entire surface of the eggs against a hard surface to

crack the shells. Peel away the shells carefully.

- Toast the bread: Toast the whole-wheat bread to your desired level of crispness.
- Assemble and enjoy: Slice the eggs in half or quarters, if desired. Place them on the toasted bread and top with your favorite ingredients. Sprinkle with salt and pepper, to taste.

Nutrition per serving (approximate):
- Calories: 300-350
- Fat: 15-20g (depending on toppings)
- Carbohydrates: 30-35g
- Fiber: 5-7g
- Protein: 20-25g
- Sodium: 200-300mg (depending on toppings)

Tips:
- For a softer yolk, cook the eggs for 9-11 minutes instead of 12.
- Add a drizzle of olive oil or balsamic vinegar to the toast for extra flavor.
- Use an egg slicer for perfectly even and uniform egg slices.
- Get creative with your toppings! This snack is adaptable to many different tastes and preferences.

Fruits & Yogurt:

Berry parfait with Greek yogurt and granola:

Ingredients (makes 1 serving):

- 1/2 cup plain Greek yogurt (2% or nonfat)
- 1/2 cup fresh berries (blueberries, raspberries, strawberries, etc.)
- 1/4 cup granola (choose a low-sugar option)
- 1/4 teaspoon chia seeds (optional)
- Honey or maple syrup (optional, to taste)
- Fresh mint leaves, for garnish (optional)

Instructions:

- Prep your berries: Wash and dry the berries. You can leave them whole, slice them, or mix different types for a vibrant combination.
- Layer the parfait: In a glass or bowl, add half of the Greek yogurt. Top with half of the berries and sprinkle with half of the granola. Repeat with the remaining yogurt, berries, and granola.
- Add toppings and adjust sweetness (optional): Sprinkle with chia seeds for extra fiber. Drizzle with a little honey or maple syrup if desired, tasting first as the berries may already be sweet. Garnish with fresh mint leaves for a refreshing touch.

- Enjoy immediately! The granola will soften over time, so it's best to eat the parfait right away.

Nutrition per serving (approximate):

- Calories: 250-300
- Fat: 5-10g
- Carbohydrates: 30-35g
- Fiber: 5-7g
- Protein: 20-25g
- Sodium: 150-200mg

Tips:

- Use any type of fresh berry you like. Frozen berries can also be used, but let them thaw slightly before adding them to the parfait.
- Choose a low-sugar granola to keep the overall sugar content moderate. You can even make your own granola with your favorite nuts and seeds.
- Don't be afraid to get creative with toppings! Add a dollop of nut butter, a drizzle of balsamic glaze, or a sprinkle of chopped nuts or seeds for an extra flavor boost.
- Portion control is key. This recipe makes one serving, but you can easily adjust the quantities to feed more people or make a larger batch for meal prepping.

Sliced pears with ricotta cheese and honey:

Ingredients (serves 2):
- 2 ripe pears
- 1/2 cup ricotta cheese
- 2 tablespoons honey
- 1/4 teaspoon vanilla extract (optional)
- Lemon juice (optional), for preventing browning
- Fresh mint leaves, for garnish (optional)

Instructions:
- Wash and dry the pears.
- Slice the pears thinly (about 1/4 inch thick) and arrange them on a plate or in individual bowls.
- Dollop ricotta cheese onto the pears, leaving some space between each dollop.
- Drizzle honey over the pears and ricotta cheese.
- (Optional) Add a few drops of vanilla extract for an extra layer of flavor.
- (Optional) Squeeze a little lemon juice on the pears to prevent browning if you're not serving them immediately.
- Garnish with fresh mint leaves for an added touch of color and flavor.

Nutrition per serving (approximate):
- Calories: 250-300
- Fat: 10-15g
- Carbohydrates: 35-40g
- Fiber: 5-7g
- Protein: 10-12g
- Sodium: 150-200mg

Tips:
- For a richer flavor, toast the walnuts or pecans in a dry pan before adding them to the dish.
- You can substitute ricotta cheese with cottage cheese or Greek yogurt for a slightly lighter option.
- Add a touch of cinnamon or nutmeg for additional warmth and spice.
- For a more elegant presentation, drizzle the dessert with balsamic glaze instead of honey.
- This recipe is easily adaptable to other fruits like apples, peaches, or plums

Frozen yogurt bark with berries and nuts:

Ingredients:
- 2 cups plain Greek yogurt (choose low-fat or full-fat based on your preference)
- 1/4 cup honey or maple syrup (optional, adjust for desired sweetness)
- 1/2 teaspoon vanilla extract
- 1/2 cup fresh or frozen berries (blueberries, raspberries, strawberries, etc.)
- 1/4 cup chopped nuts (almonds, walnuts, pistachios, etc.)
- Pinch of sea salt (optional)

Instructions:

- Line a baking sheet with parchment paper. This will make it easy to remove the frozen bark later.
- In a bowl, whisk together yogurt, honey or maple syrup (if using), and vanilla extract. This creates the base for your yogurt bark.
- Spread the yogurt mixture evenly onto the prepared baking sheet. Aim for a thickness of about 1/2 inch.
- Top with your favorite berries and chopped nuts. Get creative and arrange them in any pattern you like!
- Sprinkle with a pinch of sea salt (optional) for a touch of savory contrast.
- Freeze for at least 3 hours, or until the yogurt is completely solid.
- Once frozen, break the bark into pieces and enjoy! Store any leftover bark in the freezer for up to 2 weeks.

Nutrition per serving (approximate):
- Calories: 150-200 (depending on ingredients used)
- Fat: 5-10g
- Carbohydrates: 20-25g
- Fiber: 2-3g
- Protein: 10-15g
- Sodium: 100-150mg

Tips:
- Use your favorite fruits and nuts! Mango, cherries, and dried cranberries are also great options.
- Add a bit of shredded coconut or dark chocolate chips for extra flavor and texture.
- Drizzle with melted dark chocolate before freezing for a decadent touch.
- If your yogurt is too thick, you can thin it out with a splash of milk or plant-based milk.
- Serve with fresh fruit slices or drizzle with a touch of honey for an extra refreshing treat

Fruit salad with chia seeds and coconut flakes:

Ingredients (serves 4):
- 2 cups mixed berries (strawberries, blueberries, raspberries, etc.)
- 1 cup chopped mango
- 1 cup chopped pineapple
- 1/2 cup chopped kiwi
- 1/4 cup sliced almonds (optional)
- 2 tablespoons chia seeds
- 2 tablespoons unsweetened shredded coconut
- 1 tablespoon honey (optional)
- 1/4 teaspoon vanilla extract
- Pinch of cinnamon

Instructions:
- In a large bowl, combine the berries, mango, pineapple, and kiwi.
- Toast the almonds in a dry pan over medium heat, stirring frequently, until golden brown. Set aside to cool.
- In a small bowl, whisk together the chia seeds, coconut flakes, honey (if using), vanilla extract, and cinnamon.

- Pour the chia seed mixture over the fruit and gently toss to coat. Cover and let sit in the refrigerator for at least 20 minutes, or until the chia seeds have plumped and the fruit juices have blended.
- Divide the fruit salad among individual bowls and top with toasted almonds (if using). Enjoy immediately!

Nutrition per serving (approximate):
- Calories: 200-250
- Fat: 10-15g
- Carbohydrates: 30-35g
- Fiber: 5-7g
- Protein: 4-5g

- Sodium: 20-40mg

Tips:
- Feel free to customize this recipe by using your favorite fruits.
- For a thicker consistency, add a teaspoon of chia gel (made by soaking 1 tablespoon chia seeds in 3 tablespoons water for 15 minutes).
- Add a dollop of Greek yogurt or ricotta cheese for extra protein and creaminess.
- Substitute coconut flakes with chopped nuts, seeds, or granola for a different flavor profile.
- Enjoy your fruit salad chilled for maximum refreshment.

Baked apples with cinnamon and nuts:

Ingredients (serves 4):
- 4 medium apples (such as Granny Smith, Honeycrisp, or Braeburn)
- 1/4 cup chopped walnuts or pecans
- 1/4 cup raisins or dried cranberries (optional)
- 2 tablespoons brown sugar
- 1 teaspoon ground cinnamon
- 1/4 teaspoon ground ginger (optional)
- 1/4 teaspoon freshly grated nutmeg (optional)
- 1 tablespoon butter, softened (optional)
- 1 tablespoon honey or maple syrup

Instructions:
- Preheat oven to 375°F (190°C).

- Wash and core the apples, leaving the bottom intact to hold the filling.
- In a small bowl, combine chopped nuts, raisins or cranberries (if using), brown sugar, cinnamon, ginger (if using), and nutmeg (if using).
- Fill each apple cavity with the nut mixture, pressing it down gently.
- Place apples in a baking dish and dot each with a small pat of butter (optional). Drizzle with honey or maple syrup.
- Bake for 40-45 minutes, or until apples are tender and filling is bubbly.
- Let cool slightly before serving.

Nutrition per serving (approximate):
- Calories: 250-300

- Fat: 5-10g
- Carbohydrates: 45-50g
- Fiber: 5-7g
- Protein: 2-3g
- Sodium: 30-40mg

Tips:

- For a softer apple, add a splash of water or apple juice to the bottom of the baking dish.
- Top with vanilla ice cream, whipped cream, or yogurt for an extra decadent treat.
- Experiment with different nut combinations, such as almonds, pistachios, or cashews.
- Add a few dried figs or dates to the filling for a richer flavor.
- For a vegan option, omit the butter and use a tablespoon of vegetable oil instead.

Veggie-Based Bowls:

Mixed green salad with grilled chicken or tofu and vinaigrette:

Ingredients (serves 4):

For the salad:
- 5 cups mixed greens (spinach, arugula, romaine, etc.)
- 1 cup cherry tomatoes, halved
- 1/2 cucumber, sliced
- 1/2 red onion, thinly sliced (optional)
- 1/4 cup crumbled feta cheese (optional)
- 1/4 cup toasted nuts or seeds (almonds, sunflower seeds, pepitas)

For the grilled chicken (per serving):
- 4 boneless, skinless chicken breasts or thighs
- 1 tablespoon olive oil
- 1/2 teaspoon salt
- 1/4 teaspoon black pepper

For the grilled tofu (per serving):
- 1/2 block extra-firm tofu, drained and pressed
- 1 tablespoon olive oil
- 1/2 teaspoon soy sauce
- 1/4 teaspoon minced garlic
- 1/4 teaspoon ginger powder

For the vinaigrette:
- 2 tablespoons olive oil
- 1 tablespoon balsamic vinegar
- 1 teaspoon Dijon mustard
- 1/4 teaspoon honey
- Salt and pepper to taste

Instructions:

Prepare the protein:
- For chicken: Preheat grill or grill pan to medium-high heat. Brush chicken with olive oil and season with salt and pepper. Grill for 3-4 minutes per side, or until cooked through. Let cool slightly and slice or shred.
- For tofu: Slice tofu into 1/2-inch thick pieces. In a bowl, combine olive oil, soy sauce, garlic, and ginger powder. Marinate tofu for at least 15 minutes. Preheat grill or grill pan to medium-high heat. Grill tofu for 2-3 minutes per side, or until golden brown and slightly crispy.

Assemble the salad:
- In a large bowl, combine mixed greens, tomatoes, cucumber, red onion (if using), feta cheese (if using), and nuts or seeds.
- To make the vinaigrette, whisk together olive oil, balsamic vinegar, Dijon mustard, and honey. Season with salt and pepper to taste.
- Drizzle the vinaigrette over the salad and toss to coat.
- Top with grilled chicken or tofu and serve immediately.

Nutrition per serving (approximate):
- With chicken: Calories: 400-450, Fat: 15-20g, Carbs: 25-30g, Fiber: 3-4g, Protein: 30-35g
- With tofu: Calories: 350-400, Fat: 10-15g, Carbs: 20-25g, Fiber: 4-5g, Protein: 25-30g

Tips:
- You can substitute grilled shrimp or other protein for the chicken or tofu.
- Add other vegetables to your liking, such as bell peppers, carrots, or avocado.
- Use different types of nuts or seeds for varying textures and flavors.
- Adjust the amount of vinaigrette to your taste.
- Leftovers can be stored in an airtight container in the refrigerator for up to 3 days.

Quinoa salad with roasted vegetables and balsamic glaze:

Ingredients (serves 4-6):

For the roasted vegetables:
- 1 medium zucchini, cubed
- 1 red bell pepper, cubed
- 1 yellow bell pepper, cubed
- 1 red onion, sliced
- 1 tablespoon olive oil
- 1/2 teaspoon dried oregano
- 1/4 teaspoon salt
- 1/4 teaspoon black pepper

For the quinoa:
- 1 cup quinoa, rinsed
- 1 1/2 cups vegetable broth or water
- 1/4 teaspoon salt

For the balsamic glaze:
- 1/4 cup balsamic vinegar
- 1 tablespoon honey or maple syrup
- 1 teaspoon Dijon mustard
- Pinch of black pepper

For the salad:
- 1/4 cup crumbled feta cheese (optional)
- 1/4 cup chopped fresh parsley (optional)
- Fresh basil leaves, for garnish (optional)

Instructions:
- Preheat oven to 400°F (200°C).
- Prepare the vegetables: toss zucchini, bell peppers, and red onion with olive oil, oregano, salt, and pepper. Spread evenly on a baking sheet and roast for 20-25 minutes, or until tender and slightly browned.
- Cook the quinoa: In a saucepan, combine rinsed quinoa, vegetable broth or water, and salt. Bring to a boil, then reduce heat, cover, and simmer for 15 minutes, or until all liquid is absorbed. Fluff with a fork and set aside.
- Make the balsamic glaze: In a small saucepan, combine balsamic vinegar, honey or maple syrup, Dijon mustard, and black pepper. Heat over medium heat until simmering and slightly thickened, about 5 minutes. Set aside.
- Assemble the salad: In a large bowl, combine cooked quinoa, roasted vegetables, and crumbled feta cheese (if using). Drizzle with balsamic glaze and toss gently to coat.
- Garnish with chopped parsley and fresh basil leaves before serving.

Nutrition per serving (approximate):
- Calories: 350-400
- Fat: 10-15g
- Carbohydrates: 50-55g
- Fiber: 5-7g
- Protein: 15-20g
- Sodium: 300-400mg

Tips:
- Substitute your favorite roasted vegetables, like broccoli, Brussels sprouts, or sweet potatoes.
- Make the salad vegan by omitting the feta cheese.
- Add chopped olives, sun-dried tomatoes, or toasted nuts for additional flavor and crunch.

Lentil soup with whole-wheat bread:

Ingredients (serves 4-6):
- For the soup:
- 1 tablespoon olive oil
- 1 onion, chopped
- 2 carrots, chopped
- 2 celery stalks, chopped
- 2 cloves garlic, minced
- 1 cup green lentils, rinsed
- 6 cups vegetable broth
- 1 (28-ounce) can crushed tomatoes
- 1 teaspoon dried thyme
- 1/2 teaspoon dried oregano
- Salt and freshly ground black pepper, to taste

For the bread:
- 2 slices whole-wheat bread, toasted (optional)

Instructions:
- Heat olive oil in a large pot or Dutch oven over medium heat. Add onion, carrot, and celery, and cook until softened, about 5 minutes.
- Add garlic and cook for 30 seconds until fragrant.
- Stir in lentils, vegetable broth, crushed tomatoes, thyme, and oregano. Season generously with salt and pepper.
- Bring the mixture to a boil, then reduce heat to low and simmer for 30-40 minutes, or until lentils are tender and the soup has thickened. Be sure to stir occasionally and adjust seasonings as needed.
- While the soup simmers, toast your whole-wheat bread slices (optional).
- Serve the hot lentil soup with toasted whole-wheat bread and enjoy!

Nutrition per serving (approximate):
- Calories: 350-400
- Fat: 10-15g
- Carbohydrates: 45-50g
- Fiber: 10-12g
- Protein: 20-25g
- Sodium: 500-600mg (depending on broth and tomato sauce)

Tips:
- Add your favorite vegetables, like potatoes, sweet potatoes, or spinach, for extra nutrition.

- Top your soup with a dollop of Greek yogurt or a drizzle of tahini for added protein and creaminess.

- Adjust the spices to your liking. Add a pinch of red pepper flakes for a touch of heat, or cumin and coriander for an earthy flavor.

Spiralized zucchini noodles with tomato sauce and meatballs:

Ingredients: (serves 4)
Ingredients:

For the meatballs:
- 1/2 pound ground turkey or beef
- 1/4 cup breadcrumbs
- 1/4 cup grated Parmesan cheese
- 1/2 teaspoon dried oregano
- 1/2 teaspoon dried basil
- 1/4 teaspoon garlic powder
- 1/4 teaspoon onion powder
- Salt and pepper to taste
- 1 tablespoon olive oil

For the tomato sauce:
- 1 tablespoon olive oil
- 1 medium onion, chopped
- 2 cloves garlic, minced
- 1 (28-ounce) can crushed tomatoes
- 1/2 cup vegetable broth
- 1/2 teaspoon dried oregano
- 1/2 teaspoon dried basil
- Salt and pepper to taste

For the zucchini noodles:
- 2-3 medium zucchini
- Fresh basil leaves, for garnish (optional)
- Parmesan cheese, grated, for serving (optional)

Instructions:
- Make the meatballs: In a large bowl, combine ground meat, breadcrumbs, Parmesan cheese, oregano, basil, garlic powder, onion powder, salt, and pepper. Mix well to form a sticky mixture.
- Roll the mixture into 12-15 small meatballs.
- Heat olive oil in a large skillet over medium heat. Add meatballs and cook until browned on all sides, about 5-7 minutes.
- While the meatballs cook, prepare the tomato sauce. In the same skillet or a separate saucepan, heat olive oil over medium heat. Add onion and cook until softened, about 5 minutes.
- Add garlic and cook for 30 seconds until fragrant.
- Stir in crushed tomatoes, vegetable broth, oregano, basil, salt, and pepper. Bring to a simmer and cook for 15-20 minutes, or until thickened.
- Add the cooked meatballs to the sauce and simmer for another 5 minutes to heat through.
- Meanwhile, spiralize the zucchini using a spiralizer or julienne tool.
- Divide the zucchini noodles among plates and top with tomato sauce and meatballs.
- Garnish with fresh basil leaves and grated Parmesan cheese, if desired.

Nutrition per serving (approximate):
- Calories: 350-400
- Fat: 15-20g
- Carbohydrates: 25-30g
- Fiber: 5-7g
- Protein: 30-35g
- Sodium: 500-600mg (depending on broth)

Tips:
- If using pre-made meatballs, simply add them to the sauce to heat through.
- You can also use other vegetables like spaghetti squash or carrots for the noodles.
- Add a pinch of red pepper flakes to the sauce for a spicy kick.

Roasted Brussels sprouts with balsamic glaze and pecans:

Ingredients (serves 4-6):
- 1 pound Brussels sprouts, trimmed and halved
- 2 tablespoons olive oil
- 1/2 teaspoon salt
- 1/4 teaspoon black pepper
- 1/4 cup balsamic vinegar
- 1 tablespoon brown sugar
- 1/4 cup chopped pecans
- Fresh parsley, chopped, for garnish (optional)

Instructions:
- Preheat oven to 400°F (200°C).
- Toss Brussels sprouts with olive oil, salt, and pepper in a large bowl until evenly coated.
- Spread the Brussels sprouts on a baking sheet in a single layer.
- Roast for 20-25 minutes, or until tender and lightly browned.
- While the Brussels sprouts are roasting, in a small saucepan, combine balsamic vinegar and brown sugar. Bring to a simmer over medium heat and cook for 5-7 minutes, or until the mixture thickens slightly.
- Once the Brussels sprouts are roasted, remove them from the oven and drizzle with the balsamic glaze.
- Toss with chopped pecans and garnish with fresh parsley, if desired.

Nutrition per serving (approximate):
- Calories: 150-175
- Fat: 10-12g
- Carbohydrates: 15-18g
- Fiber: 4-5g
- Protein: 3-4g
- Sodium: 150-200mg

Tips:
- For extra flavor, add a sprinkle of garlic powder or chili flakes to the Brussels sprouts before roasting.
- If you don't have balsamic vinegar, you can substitute cider vinegar or red wine vinegar.
- You can also roast the pecans beforehand for a deeper flavor.

Extras:

Air-popped popcorn with spices:

Ingredients:
- 1/3 cup whole popcorn kernels
- 1-2 tablespoons olive oil or avocado oil (optional)
- Salt, to taste
- Your choice of spices:
- Savory: chili powder, paprika, garlic powder, onion powder, cayenne pepper, black pepper, curry powder
- Sweet: cinnamon, nutmeg, ginger, allspice, cocoa powder
- Other: nutritional yeast, dried herbs, everything bagel seasoning, nutritional yeast, lemon zest

Instructions:
- Heat the oil (if using) in a large pot or popcorn maker over medium heat.
- Add the popcorn kernels and cover with a lid.
- Shake the pot periodically until the popping slows down significantly (about 3-5 minutes).
- Remove from heat and pour the popcorn into a large bowl.
- Sprinkle with salt and your chosen spices, to taste.
- Toss well to coat and enjoy!

Nutrition per serving (approximate):
- Calories: 150-200
- Fat: 5-10g (depending on oil used)
- Carbohydrates: 20-25g
- Fiber: 3-4g
- Protein: 3-4g
- Sodium: 300-400mg (depending on salt added)

Tips:
- For a lighter option, skip the oil and popcorn in a hot air popper.
- Experiment with different spice combinations to find your favorites.
- Add other toppings like nuts, seeds, dried fruit, or cheese for extra flavor and texture.
- Store leftover popcorn in an airtight container at room temperature for up to 2 days.

Dark chocolate with nuts and dried fruit:

Ingredients:
- 12 ounces high-quality dark chocolate (70% or higher cacao content recommended)
- 1/3 cup chopped nuts (almonds, pecans, walnuts, hazelnuts, pistachios, etc.)
- 1/3 cup dried fruit (cranberries, apricots, cherries, raisins, figs, etc.)
- Optional toppings: Flaky sea salt, dried spices (cinnamon, chili flakes), coconut flakes, edible flowers

Instructions:
- Line a baking sheet with parchment paper.

- Break the chocolate into smaller pieces and place in a heatproof bowl.
- Choose your melting method:
  - Double boiler: Fill a saucepan with a few inches of water and bring to a simmer. Place the bowl with chocolate over the simmering water without touching the water, and stir until melted.
  - Microwave: Melt chocolate in 30-second intervals, stirring between each interval, until melted and smooth. Be careful not to overheat.
- Pour the melted chocolate onto the prepared baking sheet and spread evenly into a thin layer using a spatula.
- Immediately sprinkle the chopped nuts and dried fruit over the chocolate. You can arrange them in patterns or keep it random, according to your preference.
- Gently tap the baking sheet to settle the ingredients and remove any air bubbles.
- Refrigerate for at least 2 hours, or until the chocolate is completely set and firm.
- Once set, break the chocolate bark into pieces using your hands or a sharp knife.
- Optional: Drizzle with melted chocolate in a contrasting color, sprinkle with sea salt or your chosen toppings, and refrigerate until set again.

Nutrition per serving (approximate):
This recipe makes roughly 12-15 servings, depending on how thick you spread the chocolate. Each serving (estimated at 1 ounce or 28 grams) will provide:
- Calories: 180-200
- Fat: 12-14g
- Carbohydrates: 18-20g
- Fiber: 3-4g
- Protein: 2-3g
- Sodium: 30-40mg

Tips:
- Choose roasted and salted nuts for an extra flavor boost.
- Toast the nuts and dried fruit lightly for a deeper flavor and crunch.
- Use a variety of colors and textures in your toppings for visual appeal.
- Store the chocolate bark in an airtight container in the refrigerator for up to 2 weeks.
- Get creative! Play with different nuts, fruits, spices, and toppings to personalize your perfect chocolate bark.

Homemade trail mix with nuts, seeds, and dried fruit: Your Customizable & Nutritious Powerhouse Snack

Ingredients:

Base (choose 2-3 cups):

- Almonds
- Walnuts
- Cashews
- Dried cranberries
- Raisins
- Dried apricots
- Pumpkin seeds
- Sunflower seeds
- Chia seeds
- Dried cherries
- Mango slices
- Coconut flakes
- Dark chocolate chips (optional)

Flavor Boosters (choose 1-2):

- Spices: cinnamon, nutmeg, ginger, chili flakes
- Dried herbs: rosemary, thyme, oregano
- Extracts: vanilla, almond, and peppermint
- Toasted coconut chips
- Dried banana chips
- Mini pretzels

Instructions:

- Preheat oven to 350°F (175°C) if using toasted nuts or seeds. Spread your chosen nuts and seeds on a baking sheet and toast for 8-10 minutes, stirring occasionally, until golden brown and fragrant. Cool completely before assembling.
- In a large bowl, combine your chosen base ingredients. Start with 2 cups of nuts and seeds, and 1 cup of dried fruit, then adjust based on your preferences.
- Add your chosen flavor boosters, if using. Start with small amounts and adjust to taste.
- Mix everything together until it is well combined.
- Store your trail mix in an airtight container at room temperature for up to 2 weeks.

Nutrition per serving (approximate):

- Calories: 300-400 (depending on ingredients and portion size)
- Fat: 15-20g
- Carbohydrates: 30-35g
- Fiber: 5-7g
- Protein: 5-7g
- Sodium: 100-150mg

Tips:

- Experiment with different combinations of ingredients to find your perfect mix.
- Add a dash of olive oil or honey for extra flavor and binding.
- Portion your trail mix into individual bags for grab-and-go convenience.
- Use airtight containers to prevent your trail mix from becoming stale.
- Adjust the sweetness level based on your preferences.
- Be mindful of portion sizes; even healthy snacks can pack in calories.

Roasted Sweet Potato Wedges with Herbs: A Delicious & Healthy Side Dish

Ingredients (yields 4-6 servings):

- 2 large sweet potatoes, peeled and cut into wedges about 1/2 inch thick
- 2 tablespoons olive oil
- 1/2 teaspoon garlic powder
- 1/2 teaspoon smoked paprika
- 1/4 teaspoon dried thyme
- 1/4 teaspoon salt
- 1/4 teaspoon black pepper
- Freshly chopped parsley or other herbs, for garnish (optional)

Instructions:
- Preheat oven to 425°F (220°C). Line a baking sheet with parchment paper for easy cleanup.
- Wash and dry the sweet potatoes. Cut them into wedges about 1/2 inch thick and similar in size for even cooking.
- In a large bowl, toss the sweet potato wedges with olive oil, garlic powder, paprika, thyme, salt, and pepper. Make sure all the wedges are evenly coated.
- Spread the wedges in a single layer on the prepared baking sheet. Don't overcrowd the pan, as it will prevent them from crisping up.
- Roast for 20-25 minutes, or until the wedges are golden brown and tender.

on the inside, flipping halfway through the cooking time for even browning.
- Remove from the oven and let cool slightly before serving. Garnish with freshly chopped parsley or other herbs, if desired.

Nutrition per serving (approximate):
- Calories: 150-200
- Fat: 5-7g
- Carbohydrates: 25-30g
- Fiber: 3-4g
- Protein: 1-2g
- Sodium: 150-200mg (depending on salt used)

Tips:
- For extra crispy wedges, preheat the baking sheet before adding the potatoes.
- Add a pinch of cayenne pepper for a kick of heat.
- Sprinkle with grated Parmesan cheese before serving for a cheesy twist.
- Roast other vegetables on the same pan, like onions, bell peppers, or Brussels sprouts, for a colorful and flavorful side dish.

Yogurt bark with sliced vegetables and herbs:

Ingredients (makes 12-15 pieces):
- 1 cup plain Greek yogurt
- 1/4 cup honey (or maple syrup)
- 1/2 teaspoon vanilla extract
- 1/4 cup chopped cucumbers
- 1/4 cup chopped bell peppers (red, yellow, or orange)
- 1/4 cup chopped cherry tomatoes
- 1/4 cup chopped fresh dill
- 1/4 cup chopped fresh parsley
- Pinch of sea salt and black pepper

Instructions:

- Line a baking sheet with parchment paper.
- In a bowl, whisk together Greek yogurt, honey (or maple syrup), and vanilla extract until smooth.
- Divide the yogurt mixture evenly between two small bowls.
- To one bowl, add the chopped cucumbers and dill. To the other bowl, add the chopped bell peppers, cherry tomatoes, and parsley.
- Pour each yogurt mixture onto opposite sides of the baking sheet, spreading it evenly with a spatula. You can create swirls or patterns if desired.
- Sprinkle both sides with a pinch of sea salt and black pepper.
- Freeze for at least 3 hours, or until solid.
- Once frozen, break the bark into bite-sized pieces and enjoy!

Nutrition per serving (approximate):

- Calories: 100-120
- Fat: 3-4g
- Carbohydrates: 15-18g
- Fiber: 1-2g
- Protein: 5-6g
- Sodium: 100-150mg

Tips:

- Feel free to experiment with different vegetables and herbs based on your preference. Try chopped green onions, zucchini, radishes, or spinach.
- Add a pinch of chili flakes for a spicy kick.
- Drizzle with a few drops of olive oil or balsamic glaze for extra flavor.
- Store leftover bark in an airtight container in the freezer for up to 2 weeks.

Bonus Resources:

3O-Day Meal Plan For Type 2 Diabetes Management

	Breakfast	Lunch	Dinner
Day 1	Overnight Oats with Chia Seeds & Fruit, Coffee	Mediterranean Chickpea Salad with whole-wheat pita bread and olive oil drizzle.	One-Pan Chicken Fajitas
Day 2	Greek Yogurt Parfait with Berries & Granola, Green Smoothie with Spinach & Banana	Leftover Chickpea Salad with mixed greens and a light balsamic vinaigrette.	Creamy Tomato Pasta with Spinach
Day 3	Whole-Wheat English Muffins with Avocado & Poached Egg, Cottage Cheese with Sliced Cucumbers & Herbs	Southwest Fiesta Salad with grilled chicken breast and avocado wedges.	Salmon with Lemon & Broccoli
Day 4	Breakfast Burrito with Scrambled Eggs & Veggies, Hard-boiled Eggs with Whole-Wheat Toast & Avocado	Asian Noodle Salad with Peanut Dressing and shrimp (use reduced-fat peanut butter).	Turkey Burgers with Sweet Potato Fries
Day 5	Smoothie Bowl with Greek Yogurt, Granola & Nuts, Trail Mix with Yogurt & Honey	Creamy Tomato Bisque with a whole-wheat bread roll and steamed broccoli.	Pizza Night: Choose your favorite option from
Day 6	Whole-Wheat Waffles with Greek Yogurt & Berries, Fruit Salad with Coconut Yogurt & Granola	Leftover Bisque with a side salad and chopped walnuts.	Slow Cooker Honey Garlic Chicken & Veggies
Day 7	Chia Seed Pudding	Grilled Portobello	Pulled Pork Tacos with

	with Almond Milk & Fruit, Coffee	Mushroom with Goat Cheese and arugula on whole-wheat toast.	Cilantro Lime Slaw
Day 8	Cottage Cheese Toast with Sliced Tomatoes & Herbs, Scrambled Eggs with Spinach & Toast	Quinoa & Grilled Chicken Salad with lemon-tahini dressing and bell peppers.	Lentil & Vegetable Soup with whole-wheat bread
Day 9	Baked Sweet Potato Toast with Toasted Nuts & Honey, Green Smoothie with Spinach & Pear	Leftover Quinoa Salad with cucumber slices and cottage cheese	Beef Chili with a side salad
Day 10	Greek Yogurt Parfait with Berries & Granola, Oatmeal with Berries and Walnuts	Turkey & Cranberry Wraps with spinach and hummus on whole-wheat tortillas.	Chicken Curry with Coconut Milk with brown rice
Day 11	Breakfast Burrito with Tofu Scramble & Veggies, Hard-boiled Eggs with Whole-Wheat Toast & Tomato slices	Black Bean Soup with Avocado Salsa and a side of whole-wheat crackers.	Stir-Fried Chicken & Veggies with quinoa
Day 12	Smoothie Bowl with Greek Yogurt, Granola & Pumpkin Seeds, Cottage Cheese with Sliced Apples & Cinnamon	Lemon Chicken with Asparagus and quinoa (roasted on one pan).	Taco Tuesday with a Twist: Choose your favorite flavor variation from
Day 13	Whole-Wheat Pancakes with Berries & Yogurt, Fruit Salad with Coconut Yogurt & Granola	Vegetarian Pita Pockets with roasted vegetables, hummus, and crumbled feta cheese	Pasta Primavera with Spring Veggies
Day 14	Overnight Oats with Chia Seeds & Mango, Coffee	Sheet Pan Salmon with Veggies and roasted sweet potato wedges.	Mediterranean Salmon with Lemon & Herbs with roasted potatoes

Day 15	Scrambled Eggs with Smoked Salmon & Whole-Wheat Toast, Cottage Cheese with Sliced Peaches & Basil	Salmon & Veggie Leftovers with a quinoa bowl and tahini dressing.	Sheet Pan Fajita Bowls with avocado salsa
Day 16	Protein Bar with Fruit & Greek Yogurt, Green Smoothie with Spinach & Kiwi	Spicy Lentil Stew with whole-wheat bread for dipping.	Beef & Broccoli Stir-Fry
Day 17	Greek Yogurt Parfait with Blueberries & Granola, Whole-Wheat Bagel with Cream Cheese & Cucumber	Tuna Salad Lettuce Wraps with chopped apples and celery.	Chicken Pot Pie with a side salad
Day 18	Breakfast Burrito with Black Beans & Veggies, Hard-boiled Eggs with Sprouted Wheat Toast & Avocado	Buddha Bowl with Quinoa & Tahini Dressing, chickpeas, roasted Brussels sprouts, and sliced avocado	Sheet Pan Roasted Chicken & Vegetables
Day 19	Smoothie Bowl with Greek Yogurt, Granola & Almonds, Trail Mix with Yogurt & Dried Cranberries	Caprese Salad with Grilled Halloumi and sliced cucumbers on whole-wheat bread.	Lentil Shepherd's Pie
Day 20	Baked Sweet Potato Toast with Black Beans & Salsa, Scrambled Eggs with Spinach & Toast	Thai Shrimp Curry with brown rice and steamed bok choy.	Black Bean Burgers (choose your version from p. 91) on whole-wheat buns
Day 21	Chia Seed Pudding with Almond Milk & Berries, Coffee	Chicken Caesar Salad Wraps with grilled chicken breast and low-fat Caesar dressing.	Tofu Scramble with Veggies with whole-wheat toast
Day 22	Whole-Wheat English Muffins with Scrambled Eggs & Cheese, Cottage Cheese with Sliced Grapes & Mint	Hummus Veggie Wraps with whole-wheat tortillas, bell peppers, cucumbers, and spinach.	Leftovers or repeat a favorite from the previous weeks

Day 23	Nut Butter & Banana Sandwich on Whole-Wheat Bread, Green Smoothie with Spinach & Pineapple	Chicken Pot Pie Soup with a side salad and whole-wheat crackers.	Honey Garlic Chicken & Veggies
Day 24	Greek Yogurt Parfait with Peaches & Granola, Oatmeal with Apples and Pecans	Italian Meatballs with Zucchini Noodles and a side of marinara sauce.	Salmon with Lemon & Broccoli
Day 25	Breakfast Burrito with Lentil Scramble & Veggies, Hard-boiled Eggs with Whole-Wheat Toast & Hummus	Moroccan Chicken Tagine with whole-wheat couscous and steamed kale.	Creamy Tomato Pasta with Spinach
Day 26	Smoothie Bowl with Greek Yogurt, Granola & Chia Seeds, Edamame Pods with Sea Salt & Sriracha	Korean Bibimbap Bowls with brown rice, ground turkey, sauteed vegetables, and a fried egg.	Tofu Scramble with Veggies
Day 27	Baked Sweet Potato Toast with Spinach & Feta, Scrambled Eggs with Onion & Peppers	Tuna Salad Lettuce Wraps	Chicken Curry with Coconut Milk
Day 28	Choose your favorites from the previous weeks or experiment with new combinations	Caprese Salad with Grilled Halloumi	Mediterranean Salmon with Lemon & Herbs
Day 29	Scrambled Eggs with Spinach and Toast, Fruit Salad with Coconut Yogurt & Granola	Thai Shrimp Curry	Leftovers or try a new recipe from the cookbook
Day 30	Cottage Cheese Toast with Sliced Tomatoes & Herbs, Scrambled Eggs with Spinach & Toast	Italian Meatballs with Zucchini Noodles	Beef & Broccoli Stir-Fry with brown rice

Remember:

- This is just a sample plan, feel free to adapt it to your preferences and dietary needs.
- Use leftovers for lunch the next day to save time.
- Pack snacks like nuts, fruits, or yogurt to keep you fueled until dinner.
- Drink plenty of water throughout the day.
- Most importantly, enjoy your delicious and healthy meals!

Bonus Tips:

- Utilize slow cooker recipes for convenient lunches on busy days.
- Invest in reusable containers and lunch bags to reduce waste.
- Get creative with leftovers! Leftover roasted vegetables can be added to wraps or salads, and leftover grilled chicken or fish can be incorporated into sandwiches or bowls.
- Make meal prep fun! Set aside some time on the weekend to chop vegetables, cook grains, and portion out ingredients for the week ahead.

8-Week Grocery List for Diabetes Management (Flexible Guideline)

Week 1:
- Fruits: berries, apples, pears, oranges, grapefruit
- Vegetables: broccoli, spinach, kale, carrots, potatoes (sweet & regular)
- Protein: chicken breast, salmon, lean ground turkey, eggs, tofu
- Dairy: Greek yogurt, low-fat cottage cheese, unsweetened almond milk
- Grains: whole-wheat bread, brown rice, quinoa, oatmeal
- Healthy fats: avocados, olive oil, nuts and seeds

Week 2:
- Fruits: melons, grapes, plums, cherries, bananas
- Vegetables: bell peppers, mushrooms, onions, asparagus, green beans
- Protein: lean beef, shrimp, tuna, black beans, lentils
- Dairy: low-fat ricotta cheese, kefir, unsweetened coconut milk
- Grains: whole-wheat crackers, barley, farro, pita bread
- Healthy fats: peanut butter, sunflower seeds, chia seeds

Week 3:
- Fruits: pineapple, kiwi, mango, blueberries, grapefruit
- Vegetables: zucchini, cauliflower, tomatoes, celery, lettuce
- Protein: turkey sausage, chicken drumsticks, cod, chickpeas, kidney beans
- Dairy: cottage cheese with chives, plain Greek yogurt, unsweetened macadamia milk
- Grains: whole-wheat pasta, bulgur wheat, wild rice, whole-wheat tortillas
- Healthy fats: flaxseeds, pumpkin seeds, nut butter

Week 4:
- Fruits: peaches, apricots, nectarines, raspberries, cranberries
- Vegetables: eggplant, okra, sweet potatoes, Brussels sprouts, cucumbers
- Protein: pork loin, ground lamb, salmon fillets, lentils, white beans
- Dairy: low-fat mozzarella cheese, string cheese, unsweetened soy milk
- Grains: quinoa salad mix, barley flakes, bulgur wheat pilaf, corn tortillas
- Healthy fats: avocados, almonds, walnuts, tahini

Week 5:
- Fruits: pears, apples, oranges, kiwis, starfruit
- Vegetables: broccoli, spinach, collard greens, mushrooms, onions
- Protein: chicken thighs, tuna salad, tofu scramble, black beans, kidney beans

- Dairy: Greek yogurt with berries, ricotta cheese with sliced tomatoes, unsweetened cashew milk
- Grains: whole-wheat bread slices, brown rice bowls, quinoa lentil salad, whole-wheat pita bread
- Healthy fats: olive oil, pumpkin seeds, chia seeds, hummus

Week 6:
- Fruits: blueberries, blackberries, cherries, bananas, grapefruits
- Vegetables: cauliflower rice, zucchini noodles, bell peppers, carrots, celery
- Protein: turkey meatballs, shrimp stir-fry, salmon burgers, chickpeas, edamame
- Dairy: low-fat cottage cheese with herbs, kefir with sliced fruit, unsweetened almond milk
- Grains: whole-wheat couscous, farro salad, oatmeal, whole-wheat crackers
- Healthy fats: avocado slices, walnuts, flaxseeds, tahini dressing

Week 7:
- Fruits: mangoes, pineapple, peaches, plums, nectarines
- Vegetables: asparagus, green beans, snap peas, cherry tomatoes, cucumbers
- Protein: baked chicken breast, cod fish tacos, lentil soup, black bean burgers, tofu stir-fry
- Dairy: Greek yogurt with granola, low-fat mozzarella cheese, unsweetened coconut milk
- Grains: whole-wheat pasta salad, barley porridge, brown rice pilaf, whole-wheat pita bread
- Healthy fats: pumpkin seeds, sunflower seeds, olive oil, nut butter

Week 8:
- Fruits: raspberries, blackberries, strawberries, kiwi, and oranges
- Vegetables: spinach, kale, arugula, carrots, onions
- Protein: baked salmon, chicken fajitas, lentil stew, kidney bean salad, tofu scramble
- Dairy: cottage cheese with sliced cucumbers, low-fat feta cheese, unsweetened soy milk
- Grains: quinoa salad, bulgur wheat chili, whole-wheat bread slices, brown rice bowls
- Healthy fats: avocados, almonds, walnuts, and chia seeds

Additional Tips:
- Stock up on pantry staples like olive oil, spices, herbs, vinegar, and unsweetened nut butter.
- Buy frozen fruits and vegetables for convenience and affordability.
- Choose lean protein sources and limit processed meats.
- Opt for whole grains over refined grains.
- Limit sugary drinks and choose water, unsweetened tea, or black coffee.
- Enjoy snacks like nuts, seeds, yogurt, or fruits in between meals.

Here are some additional ideas to personalize your grocery list:

- Include ethnic ingredients: If you enjoy Italian food, stock up on whole-wheat pasta, tomato sauce, and fresh herbs. For Asian cuisine, consider brown rice, stir-fry vegetables, and low-sodium soy sauce.
- Explore plant-based options: Experiment with different types of tofu, tempeh, and vegan protein sources. Add protein-rich lentils, beans, and quinoa to your meals.
- Focus on seasonal produce: Enjoy the freshest and most flavorful fruits and vegetables by choosing what's in season. Local farmers' markets are a great way to find seasonal produce and support local growers.
- Don't forget healthy fats: Avocados, nuts, seeds, and olive oil are essential for satiety and provide important nutrients. Include them in your meals and snacks in moderation.
- Plan your meals for the week: Make a meal plan to help you stay on track and avoid unhealthy impulse purchases at the grocery store. This will also help you use up ingredients effectively and minimize food waste.

Remember, managing diabetes is a continuous journey. This grocery list is a tool to guide you towards healthy choices, but it's important to listen to your body and adjust your diet as needed. Consult with your doctor or a registered dietitian for personalized advice and support.

Happy and healthy shopping!

Festive Holiday Recipes for Diverse Dietary Needs:

Vegan & Delicious:

Lentil Shepherd's Pie with Butternut Squash Mash: A Hearty & Vegan Holiday Treat
Ingredients:
For the lentil filling:

- 1 tablespoon olive oil
- 1 onion, chopped
- 2 carrots, chopped
- 2 celery stalks, chopped
- 2 cloves garlic, minced
- 1 cup green lentils, rinsed
- 4 cups vegetable broth
- 1 (14.5 oz) can diced tomatoes, undrained
- 1 tablespoon tomato paste
- 1 teaspoon dried thyme
- 1/2 teaspoon dried rosemary
- Salt and black pepper to taste

For the butternut squash mash:

- 1 medium butternut squash, peeled and cubed
- 1 tablespoon olive oil
- Salt and black pepper to taste

To finish:

- 1 tablespoon vegan butter (optional)
- Fresh parsley, chopped, for garnish (optional)

Instructions:

- Preheat the oven to 400°F (200°C).
- Heat olive oil in a large Dutch oven over medium heat. Add onion, carrots, and celery, and cook until softened, about 5 minutes.
- Stir in garlic and cook for 30 seconds, until fragrant.
- Add lentils, broth, diced tomatoes, tomato paste, thyme, and rosemary.

Season with salt and pepper to taste. Bring to a simmer, then cover and reduce heat to low.

- Simmer for 20-25 minutes, or until lentils are tender.
- While the lentils cook, prepare the butternut squash mash. Place cubed squash on a baking sheet, drizzle with olive oil, and season with salt and pepper. Roast for 30-35 minutes, or until tender and fork-pierceable.
- Once the lentils are cooked, transfer them to a baking dish or individual ramekins. Mash the roasted butternut squash with a fork or potato masher, and spread it evenly over the lentil filling.
- (Optional) Dot the top of the mash with vegan butter for a richer flavor.
- Bake for 15-20 minutes, or until the mash is golden brown and heated through.
- Garnish with fresh parsley, if desired, and serve immediately.

Nutrition per serving (approximate):

- Calories: 450-500
- Fat: 15-20g
- Carbohydrates: 60-65g
- Fiber: 10-12g
- Protein: 20-25g
- Sodium: 500-600mg (depending on broth)

Tips:
- Leftovers can be stored in an airtight container in the refrigerator for up to 3 days.

- Add a diced potato to the lentil filling for extra heartiness.
- Use your favorite herbs and spices to customize the flavor.
- Top with vegan Parmesan cheese for a cheesy twist.

Spicy Black Bean Burgers with Chipotle Mayo:
Ingredients (makes 8 patties):

For the black bean burgers:
- 1 (15-ounce) can black beans, drained and rinsed
- 1/2 red bell pepper, finely chopped
- 1/2 cup scallions, finely chopped
- 3 tablespoons fresh cilantro, chopped
- 3 garlic cloves, minced
- 1/2 cup quick-cooking oats
- 1 large egg
- 1 teaspoon cayenne pepper hot sauce
- 1 tablespoon ground cumin
- 1/4 teaspoon kosher salt
- Cooking spray or oil mister

For the chipotle mayo:
1/2 cup mayonnaise
- 1 tablespoon chipotle peppers in adobo sauce (more for extra spice)
- 1 teaspoon adobo sauce from the can
- Pinch of kosher salt

Instructions:
- Make the black bean burgers: In a large bowl, mash the black beans with a fork until slightly chunky.
- Add the bell pepper, scallions, cilantro, garlic, oats, egg, hot sauce, cumin, and salt. Mix well to combine.
- Form the mixture into 8 equal patties.

- Make the chipotle mayo: In a small bowl, whisk together the mayonnaise, chipotle peppers, adobo sauce, and salt. Set aside.
- Cook the burgers: Heat a grill pan or skillet over medium heat. Lightly spray with cooking spray or oil mister. Cook the burgers for 4-5 minutes per side, or until golden brown and cooked through.
- Assemble and serve: Toast burger buns (optional). Spread each bun with chipotle mayo, top with a burger patty, and your desired toppings (lettuce, tomato, onion, avocado, etc.). Enjoy!

Nutrition per serving (approximate):
- Calories: 250-300
- Fat: 10-15g
- Carbohydrates: 30-35g
- Fiber: 5-7g
- Protein: 15-20g
- Sodium: 400-500mg (depending on ingredients)

Tips:
- You can use pre-cooked black beans to save time.
- Make the chipotle mayo ahead of time and store it in the refrigerator for up to 3 days.

- Add other spices to the black bean mixture, such as smoked paprika or chili powder, for extra flavor.

- Serve the burgers with your favorite burger toppings and sides.

Creamy Vegan Mushroom Stroganoff:

Ingredients (serves 4-6):

For the sauce:
- 1 cup raw cashews, soaked for at least 2 hours or overnight
- 1 cup unsweetened plant-based milk (almond, soy, or oat milk)
- 1/2 cup nutritional yeast
- 2 tablespoons Dijon mustard
- 1 tablespoon lemon juice
- 1 clove garlic, minced
- 1/2 teaspoon dried thyme
- Salt and black pepper to taste

For the stroganoff:
- 1 tablespoon olive oil
- 1 onion, diced
- 1 large portobello mushroom, chopped
- 8 ounces cremini or button mushrooms, sliced
- 2 cloves garlic, minced
- 1 cup dry white wine (optional)
- 1 1/2 cups vegetable broth
- 1 teaspoon smoked paprika
- 1/2 teaspoon dried oregano
- Fresh parsley, chopped, for garnish

Instructions:
- Make the sauce: Drain the soaked cashews and blend them with the plant-based milk, nutritional yeast, Dijon mustard, lemon juice, garlic, thyme, salt, and pepper in a high-powered blender until smooth and creamy. Set aside.

- Cook the vegetables: Heat olive oil in a large skillet or Dutch oven over medium heat. Add the onion and cook until softened, about 5 minutes.
- Add the portobello and cremini mushrooms and cook for another 5-7 minutes, or until browned and softened. Stir in the garlic and cook for 30 seconds until fragrant.
- Deglaze (optional): If using, pour in the white wine and scrape up any browned bits from the bottom of the pan. Let simmer for 2-3 minutes.
- Add broth and seasonings: Pour in the vegetable broth, paprika, and oregano. Bring to a simmer and cook for 5 minutes.
- Stir in sauce and simmer: Gently stir in the cashew sauce and simmer for 5-7 minutes more, until heated through. Season with additional salt and pepper if needed.
- Serve: Garnish with chopped parsley and serve over your favorite cooked pasta, quinoa, or brown rice.

Nutrition per serving (approximate):
- Calories: 400-450
- Fat: 15-20g
- Carbohydrates: 40-45g
- Fiber: 5-6g
- Protein: 20-25g
- Sodium: 600-700mg (depending on broth and soy sauce)

Tips:

- For a thinner sauce, add a bit more vegetable broth or plant-based milk.

- To make this recipe gluten-free, use certified gluten-free pasta or quinoa.
- You can add other vegetables to the stroganoff, such as peas, carrots, or spinach

Roasted Brussels Sprouts with Pecans and Cranberries: A Sweet & Savory Holiday Side

Ingredients:

- 1 1/2 pounds Brussels sprouts, trimmed and halved
- 2 tablespoons olive oil
- 1/2 teaspoon salt
- 1/4 teaspoon black pepper
- 1/2 cup chopped pecans
- 1/4 cup dried cranberries
- 1 tablespoon maple syrup (optional)
- Fresh thyme leaves, for garnish (optional)

Instructions:

- Preheat the oven to 400°F (200°C).
- Toss the Brussels sprouts, olive oil, salt, and pepper in a large bowl until evenly coated. Spread them out on a baking sheet in a single layer.
- Roast for 20-25 minutes, or until the Brussels sprouts are tender and slightly browned.
- While the Brussels sprouts are roasting, toast the pecans in a dry skillet over medium heat until fragrant and slightly browned, about 3-5 minutes. Set aside.
- In a small saucepan, combine the cranberries and maple syrup (if using) over low heat. Simmer for 2-3

minutes, until the cranberries soften, and the syrup thickens slightly.

- Once the Brussels sprouts are roasted, remove them from the oven and immediately toss them with the toasted pecans and cranberry mixture.
- Garnish with fresh thyme leaves (optional) and serve warm.

Nutrition per serving (approximate):

- Calories: 150
- Fat: 10g
- Carbohydrates: 15g
- Fiber: 4g
- Protein: 3g
- Sodium: 150mg (depending on salt)

Tips:

- For a crispier texture, roast the Brussels sprouts for an additional 5-10 minutes.
- You can substitute walnuts or almonds for the pecans.
- Add a squeeze of fresh lemon juice for a touch of acidity.
- This recipe can be easily doubled or tripled to serve a larger crowd.

Baked Tofu Nuggets with Sweet Chili Dipping Sauce:

Ingredients:

For the Nuggets:

- 14 oz extra firm tofu, drained and pressed
- 1/4 cup nutritional yeast
- 1/4 cup cornstarch
- 1/2 teaspoon paprika
- 1/2 teaspoon garlic powder
- 1/4 teaspoon onion powder
- 1/4 teaspoon black pepper
- 1 tablespoon olive oil

For the Sweet Chili Dipping Sauce:
- 1/4 cup vegan mayo
- 2 tablespoons sweet chili sauce
- 1 tablespoon sriracha (optional, for extra spice)
- 1 teaspoon lime juice
- 1/2 teaspoon agave nectar (optional, for sweetness)

Instructions:
- Preheat the oven to 400°F (200°C). Line a baking sheet with parchment paper.
- Prepare the tofu: Crumble the pressed tofu into a large bowl. Add the nutritional yeast,cornstarch, paprika, garlic powder, onion powder, and black pepper. Toss to evenly coat the tofu.
- Shape the nuggets: Drizzle the olive oil over the tofu mixture and gently fold it in. Using your hands, form the tofu mixture into small nuggets, about the size of bite-sized chicken nuggets.
- Bake the nuggets: Place the tofu nuggets on the prepared baking sheet and bake for 20-25 minutes, or until

golden brown and crispy. Flip the nuggets halfway through baking for even browning.
- Make the dipping sauce: While the nuggets bake, whisk together the vegan mayo, sweet chili sauce, sriracha (if using), lime juice, and agave nectar (if using) in a small bowl.
- Serve: Let the tofu nuggets cool slightly before serving with the sweet chili dipping sauce. Enjoy!

Nutrition per serving (approximately, based on 10 nuggets):
- Calories: 150
- Fat: 6g
- Carbohydrates: 15g
- Fiber: 2g
- Protein: 8g
- Sodium: 250mg (depending on your ingredients)

Tips:
- For a thicker dipping sauce, add a teaspoon of cornstarch mixed with 1 tablespoon of water to the sauce and whisk until smooth before simmering for a few minutes.
- Feel free to adjust the spices in the nuggets to your taste. You can also add other herbs, like oregano or thyme.
- Serve these nuggets with other dipping sauces like tahini sauce, hummus, or marinara sauce for variety.

Low-Carb & Satisfying:

Cauliflower "Rice" Pilaf with Herbs and Nuts:

Ingredients (serves 4-6):

- 1 head cauliflower, trimmed and grated (about 8 cups)
- 1 tablespoon olive oil
- 1 medium onion, chopped
- 2 cloves garlic, minced
- 1 cup vegetable broth
- 1/4 cup chopped fresh parsley
- 1/4 cup chopped fresh basil
- 1/4 cup chopped fresh chives
- 1/4 cup chopped toasted walnuts or pecans
- 1/4 cup grated Parmesan cheese (optional)
- Salt and freshly ground black pepper, to taste
- Zest and juice of 1/2 lemon (optional)

Instructions:

- In a large skillet or Dutch oven, heat olive oil over medium heat. Add onion and cook until softened, about 5 minutes. Stir in garlic and cook for 30 seconds until fragrant.
- Add grated cauliflower and cook, stirring occasionally, until slightly softened and golden brown, about 5-7 minutes. Be careful not to overcook, or the cauliflower will become mushy.
- Pour in vegetable broth and bring to a simmer. Reduce heat to low, cover, and cook for 10-15 minutes, or until cauliflower is tender but still has a slight bite.
- Remove from heat and stir in chopped parsley, basil, chives, toasted nuts, Parmesan cheese (if using), salt, pepper, and lemon zest (if using). Squeeze in some lemon juice to taste and fluff with a fork.
- Serve immediately as a side dish, stuffing for poultry, or as part of a vegetarian main course.

Nutrition per serving (approximate):

- Calories: 150-200 (depending on added cheese and nuts)
- Fat: 8-10g
- Carbohydrates: 15-20g (mostly fiber)
- Protein: 5-7g
- Fiber: 5-7g
- Sodium: 300-400mg (depending on broth)

Tips:

- For a richer flavor, add a bay leaf to the pan while cooking the cauliflower.
- You can use other herbs, such as oregano, thyme, or rosemary, for a different flavor profile.
- Leftovers can be stored in an airtight container in the refrigerator for up to 3 days. Reheat gently in a pan or microwave.

Keto Cranberry Pecan Chicken Salad:

Ingredients:

- 2 cups cooked and shredded chicken breast (skinless and boneless)

- 1/2 cup chopped celery
- 1/4 cup chopped red onion
- 1/4 cup chopped pecans
- 1/4 cup dried cranberries
- 2 tablespoons mayonnaise (choose keto-friendly mayonnaise for a fully keto version)
- 1 tablespoon Dijon mustard
- 1 teaspoon lemon juice
- 1/4 teaspoon salt
- 1/4 teaspoon black pepper
- Optional: fresh parsley for garnish

Instructions:
- In a large bowl, combine the shredded chicken, celery, red onion, pecans, and cranberries.
- In a separate bowl, whisk together the mayonnaise, Dijon mustard, lemon juice, salt, and pepper.
- Pour the dressing over the chicken mixture and toss gently to combine.
- Taste and adjust seasonings as needed.
- Serve the chicken salad on a bed of lettuce, in lettuce wraps, or on keto-friendly crackers. Garnish with fresh parsley, if desired.

Nutrition per serving (approximate):
- Calories: 350-400
- Fat: 25-30g
- Carbohydrates: 5-7g (2-3g net carbs if using keto-friendly mayonnaise)
- Fiber: 1-2g
- Protein: 30-35g
- Sodium: 300-400mg (depending on mayonnaise and broth used)

Tips:
- You can use leftover rotisserie chicken or grill/bake your own for this recipe.
- For a creamier chicken salad, you can add a tablespoon of full-fat sour cream or cream cheese.
- Add other chopped vegetables like cucumber or bell peppers for additional flavor and nutrients.
- Make it a festive holiday starter by stuffing the salad into mini bell peppers or celery sticks.

Roasted Salmon with Brussels Sprouts and Dijon Mustard Glaze:

Ingredients (serves 4):

For the salmon:
- 4 (6-ounce) salmon fillets, skin-on
- 1 tablespoon olive oil
- 1/2 teaspoon salt
- 1/4 teaspoon black pepper

For the Brussels sprouts:
- 1 pound Brussels sprouts, trimmed and halved
- 1 tablespoon olive oil
- 1/2 teaspoon salt
- 1/4 teaspoon black pepper

For the Dijon mustard glaze:
- 2 tablespoons Dijon mustard
- 2 tablespoons honey
- 1 tablespoon apple cider vinegar
- 1 tablespoon soy sauce
- 1 teaspoon lemon juice
- 1/2 teaspoon dried thyme
- Pinch of cayenne pepper (optional)

Instructions:

- Preheat the oven to 425°F (220°C). Line a baking sheet with parchment paper.
- Prepare the salmon: Pat the salmon fillets dry with paper towels. Brush both sides with olive oil and season with salt and pepper. Place skin-side down on the prepared baking sheet.
- Prepare the Brussels sprouts: Toss the Brussels sprouts with olive oil, salt, and pepper. Arrange them around the salmon on the baking sheet.
- Make the Dijon mustard glaze: In a small bowl, whisk together Dijon mustard, honey, apple cider vinegar, soy sauce, lemon juice, thyme, and cayenne pepper (if using).
- Bake: Roast the salmon and Brussels sprouts for 15-20 minutes, or until the salmon is cooked through (flaky when tested with a fork) and the Brussels sprouts are tender. Brush the salmon with the Dijon mustard glaze during the last 5 minutes of cooking.
- Serve: Transfer the salmon and Brussels sprouts to serving plates. Drizzle with any remaining glaze and enjoy!

Nutrition per serving (approximate):

- Calories: 450-500
- Fat: 25-30g
- Carbohydrates: 25-30g
- Fiber: 5-6g
- Protein: 30-35g
- Sodium: 500-600mg (depending on soy sauce)

Tips:

- For extra crispy skin, sprinkle the salmon with a pinch of brown sugar before baking.
- You can substitute other vegetables for the Brussels sprouts, such as broccoli florets, cauliflower florets, or asparagus spears.
- This dish is also delicious served with mashed potatoes, quinoa, or brown rice.

Creamy Avocado Deviled Eggs:

Ingredients (makes 12 halves):

- 6 large hard-boiled eggs
- 1 ripe avocado, pitted and peeled
- 1/4 cup fresh lemon juice
- 1 tablespoon chopped fresh chives
- 1/4 teaspoon garlic powder
- Salt and freshly ground black pepper, to taste
- Smoked paprika, for garnish (optional)

Instructions:

- Carefully peel the hard-boiled eggs and cut them in half lengthwise. Scoop out the yolks, placing them in a medium bowl. Set the egg whites aside.
- Mash the avocado until smooth and creamy. Add the lemon juice, chives,

garlic powder, salt, and pepper to the mashed avocado. Mix well to combine.

- Using a spoon or piping bag, fill the egg white halves with the avocado mixture.
- Garnish with a sprinkle of smoked paprika, if desired. Chill for at least 30 minutes before serving.

Nutrition per serving (approximate):
- Calories: 100-120
- Fat: 8-10g (mostly healthy fats from avocado)
- Carbohydrates: 2-3g
- Fiber: 1-2g
- Protein: 3-4g
- Sodium: 50-70mg (depending on salt added)

Tips:
- For a smoother filling, blend the avocado mixture in a food processor.
- Use fresh herbs like dill or cilantro for a different flavor twist.
- Add a pinch of cayenne pepper for a subtle kick.
- Top with crumbled bacon or chopped nuts for extra texture and flavor.
- This recipe can be easily doubled or tripled for larger gatherings

Antipasto Skewers with Prosciutto, Mozzarella, and Olives:

Ingredients (makes 12 skewers):
- 12 slices prosciutto, thinly sliced
- 12 mozzarella balls, mini or bocconcini size
- 12 green olives, pitted
- 12 cherry tomatoes
- 12 fresh basil leaves (optional)
- Extra virgin olive oil, for drizzling
- Balsamic glaze, for drizzling (optional)
- Freshly ground black pepper, to taste

Instructions:
- Assemble the skewers: Thread a prosciutto slice onto a skewer. followed by a mozzarella ball, an olive, a cherry tomato, and a basil leaf (if using). Repeat with remaining ingredients to make 12 skewers.
- Drizzle with olive oil and balsamic glaze (if using). Season with black pepper to taste.
- Serve immediately at room temperature, or chill for 30 minutes for a slightly firmer texture.

Nutrition per serving (approximate):
- Calories: 200-250
- Fat: 15-20g
- Carbohydrates: 5-10g
- Fiber: 1-2g
- Protein: 10-15g
- Sodium: 400-500mg (depending on olives and prosciutto)

Tips:
- You can use any type of olive you like, such as Kalamata, Castelvetrano, or Manzanilla.

- Sun-dried tomatoes can be used instead of cherry tomatoes for a different flavor.
- Add a small piece of fresh mozzarella to the cherry tomato if using larger tomatoes.
- For a vegetarian option, substitute the prosciutto with roasted zucchini slices or marinated artichoke hearts.
- These skewers can be made ahead of time and stored in the refrigerator for up to 24 hours.

Almond Flour Pumpkin Bread with Maple Glaze:

Ingredients:

For the bread:

- 1 1/2 cups blanched almond flour
- 1/2 cup coconut flour
- 1/2 teaspoon baking soda
- 1/2 teaspoon baking powder
- 1/2 teaspoon ground cinnamon
- 1/4 teaspoon ground nutmeg
- 1/4 teaspoon ground ginger
- 1/4 teaspoon salt
- 1 cup canned pumpkin puree
- 3 large eggs
- 1/2 cup pure maple syrup
- 1/4 cup melted coconut oil

For the maple glaze:

- 1/4 cup pure maple syrup
- 1 tablespoon melted coconut oil
- 1/4 teaspoon vanilla extract

Instructions:

- Preheat the oven to 350°F (175°C). Grease a 9x5 inch loaf pan.
- In a large bowl, whisk together almond flour, coconut flour, baking soda, baking powder, cinnamon, nutmeg, ginger, and salt.
- In a separate bowl, whisk together pumpkin puree, eggs, maple syrup, and melted coconut oil until smooth.
- Pour the wet ingredients into the dry ingredients and stir until just combined. Do not overmix.
- Pour the batter into the prepared loaf pan and smooth the top.
- Bake for 50-55 minutes, or until a toothpick inserted into the center comes out clean.
- Let the bread cool in the pan for 10 minutes, then transfer it to a wire rack to cool completely.

To make the maple glaze:

- In a small bowl, whisk together maple syrup, melted coconut oil, and vanilla extract.
- Once the bread has cooled, drizzle the maple glaze over the top.

Nutrition per serving (approximate):

- Calories: 350-400
- Fat: 20-25g
- Carbohydrates: 30-35g
- Fiber: 4-5g
- Protein: 10-15g
- Sodium: 200-250mg

Tips:

- For an extra boost of flavor, add 1/2 cup chopped walnuts or pecans to the batter.
- You can also use melted butter instead of coconut oil in the batter and glaze.

Coconut Flour Cookies with Dark Chocolate Chips:

Ingredients (makes about 12 cookies):

- 1/2 cup (60g) coconut flour
- 1/4 cup (25g) almond flour
- 1/4 teaspoon baking soda
- 1/4 teaspoon salt

- 1/4 cup (50g) unsalted butter, melted and cooled slightly
- 1/4 cup (60g) granulated monk fruit sweetener or erythritol (or regular sugar, if not following keto)
- 1 large egg
- 1/2 teaspoon vanilla extract
- 1/2 cup (100g) dark chocolate chips

Instructions:
- Preheat the oven to 350°F (175°C). Line a baking sheet with parchment paper.
- In a medium bowl, whisk together coconut flour, almond flour, baking soda, and salt.
- In a separate bowl, whisk together melted butter, sweetener, egg, and vanilla extract until smooth.
- Add the wet ingredients to the dry ingredients and stir until just combined. Fold in the chocolate chips.
- Drop heaping tablespoons of dough onto the prepared baking sheet, leaving about 2 inches of space between them. The dough will spread slightly as it bakes.
- Bake for 8-10 minutes, or until the edges are golden brown. Let cool on the baking sheet for a few minutes before transferring to a wire rack to cool completely.

Nutrition per serving (approximate):
- Calories: 180-200 (depending on sweetener used)
- Fat: 13-15g
- Carbohydrates: 8-10g (net carbs: 3-5g)
- Fiber: 3-4g
- Protein: 2-3g
- Sodium: 120-150mg

Tips:
- For a chewier cookie, bake for a few minutes less.
- You can substitute other types of flour in place of the almond flour, such as oat flour or hemp flour.
- Try adding different mix-ins, such as chopped nuts, dried fruit, or spices like cinnamon or ginger.

Quinoa Stuffed Peppers with Herbs and Spices:
Ingredients (makes 4-6 servings):
For the filling:
- 1 cup quinoa, rinsed
- 1 1/2 cups vegetable broth
- 1 tablespoon olive oil
- 1/2 onion, finely chopped
- 1 clove garlic, minced
- 1 small red bell pepper, diced
- 1/2 cup chopped mushrooms
- 1/4 cup chopped fresh parsley
- 1/4 cup chopped fresh cilantro
- 1 teaspoon dried oregano
- 1/2 teaspoon ground cumin
- 1/4 teaspoon smoked paprika
- Salt and freshly ground black pepper, to taste

For the peppers:
- 4-6 bell peppers (red, orange, yellow)
- Olive oil, for brushing

Instructions:

- Preheat the oven to 400°F (200°C).
- Cook the quinoa: In a saucepan, combine the quinoa and vegetable broth. Bring to a boil, then reduce heat and simmer for 15 minutes, or until quinoa is cooked and all liquid is absorbed. Fluff with a fork and set aside.
- Prepare the filling: While the quinoa cooks, heat olive oil in a pan over medium heat. Add onion and cook until softened, about 5 minutes. Add garlic and red bell pepper, and cook for another 2-3 minutes.
- Stir in mushrooms, parsley, cilantro, oregano, cumin, paprika, salt, and pepper. Cook for 1 minute until fragrant.
- Add the cooked quinoa to the pan and mix well to combine. Taste and adjust seasonings as needed.
- Prepare the peppers: Cut the tops off the bell peppers and remove the seeds and membranes. Brush the inside of the peppers with olive oil.
- Stuff the peppers: Fill each pepper with the quinoa mixture, leaving some space at the top.
- Place the peppers upright in a baking dish, and add about 1/2 inch of water to the bottom of the dish.
- Bake for 20-25 minutes, or until peppers are tender and slightly softened.
- Serve warm, topped with additional fresh herbs, if desired.

Nutrition per serving (approximate):

- Calories: 250-300
- Fat: 8-10g
- Carbohydrates: 40-45g
- Fiber: 6-8g
- Protein: 8-10g
- Sodium: 300-400mg (depending on broth)

Tips:

- You can use any type of quinoa you like (white, black, red, etc.).
- Add other vegetables to the filling, such as chopped zucchini, carrots, or spinach.
- Use different herbs and spices to your taste.

Gluten-Free Gingerbread Cookies:

Ingredients:

Dry:

- 1 ½ cups almond flour
- 1 ¼ cup oat flour
- 1 ½ teaspoons ground ginger
- 1 teaspoon ground cinnamon
- ¼ teaspoon nutmeg
- ¼ teaspoon cloves
- 1 teaspoon baking soda
- ½ teaspoon salt

Wet:

- ½ cup unsalted butter, softened
- ½ cup light brown sugar, packed
- 1 large egg
- ¼ cup molasses
- 1 tablespoon pure vanilla extract

Optional:

- 1/2 cup chopped walnuts or pecans
- Powdered sugar, for dusting (optional)

Instructions:

- Preheat the oven to 350°F (175°C). Line a baking sheet with parchment paper.
- In a medium bowl, whisk together almond flour, oat flour, ginger, cinnamon, nutmeg, cloves, baking soda, and salt.
- In a separate bowl, cream together butter and brown sugar until light and fluffy. Beat in the egg, molasses, and vanilla extract until combined.
- Gradually add the dry ingredients to the wet ingredients, mixing until just combined. Fold in the chopped nuts (if using).
- Drop tablespoons of dough onto the prepared baking sheet, leaving space for spreading.
- Bake for 8-10 minutes, or until cookies are firm around the edges but still slightly soft in the center.
- Let cool on the baking sheet for a few minutes before transferring to a wire rack to cool completely.
- Dust with powdered sugar before serving, if desired.

Nutrition per serving (approximate, based on 12 cookies):

- Calories: 150
- Fat: 8g
- Carbohydrates: 20g
- Fiber: 2g
- Protein: 2g
- Sodium: 120mg

Tips:

- For chewier cookies, bake for less time. For crispier cookies, bake for a minute or two longer.
- You can use coconut flour instead of oat flour, but the cookies may be slightly drier.
- Add a teaspoon of grated orange zest for an extra burst of flavor.
- Store the cookies in an airtight container at room temperature for up to 3 days, or freeze for longer storage

Chocolate Avocado Mousse in Dark Chocolate Cups:

Ingredients (yields 10-12 mousse cups):

For the avocado mousse:

- 1 ripe avocado, peeled and pitted
- 1/2 cup unsweetened cocoa powder
- 1/4 cup honey or maple syrup (adjust to taste)
- 1/4 cup full-fat coconut milk
- 1/4 teaspoon vanilla extract,
- Pinch of salt

For the chocolate cups:

- 10-12 dark chocolate melting wafers or couverture chocolate

Instructions:

- Make the avocado mousse: In a food processor or blender, combine the avocado, cocoa powder, honey or maple syrup, coconut milk, vanilla extract, and salt. Blend until smooth and creamy, scraping down the sides as needed.
- Prepare the chocolate cups: Melt the chocolate wafers or couverture chocolate according to package

instructions. Using a spoon or piping bag, spread a thin layer of melted chocolate onto the inside of small silicone muffin cups or mini ramekins. Let the chocolate harden in the refrigerator for at least 15 minutes.

- Assemble the mousse cups: Once the chocolate cups are hardened, fill them with the avocado mousse using a spoon or piping bag. Smooth the top and tap gently to remove any air bubbles.

- Chill and decorate: Refrigerate the mousse cups for at least 2 hours, or overnight for a firmer texture. Before serving, you can drizzle with additional melted chocolate, sprinkle with crushed nuts, or top with a fresh berry.

Nutrition per serving (approximate):

- Calories: 150-175
- Fat: 12-15g
- Carbohydrates: 8-10g (2-3g fiber)
- Protein: 2-3g
- Sodium: 30-40mg

Tips:

- Use the ripest avocado you can find for the smoothest mousse.
- Adjust the sweetness of the mousse to your taste by adding more or less honey or maple syrup.
- You can substitute almond milk or milk of your choice for the coconut milk.
- For a dairy-free option, choose vegan dark chocolate melting wafers or couverture chocolate.
- Get creative with your toppings! Coconut flakes, chopped nuts, or a drizzle of caramel sauce are all delicious options.

Honey Glazed Ham with Rosemary and Apricots:

Ingredients:

For the glaze:

- 1/2 cup apricot preserves
- 1/4 cup honey
- 1/4 cup brown sugar
- 2 tablespoons Dijon mustard
- 2 tablespoons orange juice
- 1 tablespoon fresh rosemary, chopped (plus extra sprigs for garnish)
- 1/4 teaspoon ground cloves
- Pinch of salt

For the ham:

- 1 fully cooked bone-in ham, spiral-cut or pre-scored (7-8 pounds)
- 1/2 cup apple cider
- 2 tablespoons whole cloves

Instructions:

- Prepare the glaze: In a small saucepan, combine apricot preserves, honey, brown sugar, Dijon mustard, orange juice, chopped rosemary, ground cloves, and salt. Bring to a simmer over medium heat, stirring frequently, until the sugar dissolves and the glaze thickens slightly. Set aside.
- Preheat oven to 325°F (165°C).
- Place the ham in a roasting pan, fat side up. If using a spiral-cut ham, gently pull apart the slices slightly to create more surface area for the glaze.
- Stud the ham with whole cloves, pushing them halfway into the meat.

- Pour the apple cider into the bottom of the roasting pan. Brush the entire surface of the ham generously with the honey-apricot glaze.
- Cover the pan loosely with foil and bake for 1 hour. Baste the ham with the remaining glaze every 15-20 minutes.
- Uncover the pan and increase the oven temperature to 400°F (200°C). Bake for an additional 30-45 minutes, or until the glaze is bubbly and caramelized and the internal temperature of the ham reaches 160°F (71°C).
- Transfer the ham to a serving platter and let rest for 15-20 minutes before carving. Garnish with additional fresh rosemary sprigs, if desired.

Nutrition per serving (approximate):

- Calories: 500-600
- Fat: 30-35g
- Carbohydrates: 50-55g
- Fiber: 2-3g
- Protein: 35-40g
- Sodium: 800-1000mg (depending on ham and glaze ingredients)

Tips:

- For a spicier kick, add a pinch of cayenne pepper to the glaze.
- If the glaze thickens too much while baking, add a splash of water or orange juice to thin it out.
- Reserve any leftover glaze to serve alongside the ham for additional dipping.

Roasted Vegetable Medley with Balsamic Glaze:

Ingredients (yields approximately 4 servings):

Vegetables:

- 1 medium zucchini, chopped
- 1 red bell pepper, chopped
- 1 yellow bell pepper, chopped
- 1 red onion, sliced
- 1 head broccoli, cut into florets
- 1 medium sweet potato, peeled and diced

Glaze:

- 1/4 cup balsamic vinegar
- 1 tablespoon honey or maple syrup
- 1 teaspoon olive oil
- 1/4 teaspoon dried thyme
- Pinch of salt and pepper

Additional:

- 2 tablespoons olive oil
- Fresh rosemary sprig (optional)
- Sea salt flakes, to taste
- Freshly ground black pepper, to taste

Instructions:

- Preheat the oven to 400°F (200°C). Line a baking sheet with parchment paper.
- In a large bowl, toss the chopped vegetables with olive oil. Arrange them in a single layer on the prepared baking sheet.
- Optionally, tuck a sprig of fresh rosemary between the veggies for added aroma.
- Roast for 20-25 minutes, or until the vegetables are tender and slightly browned.
- While the vegetables roast, prepare the glaze by whisking together balsamic vinegar, honey or maple syrup, olive oil, thyme, salt, and pepper in a small saucepan.
- Bring the glaze to a simmer over medium heat and cook for 5-7 minutes, or until slightly thickened.
- Once the vegetables are roasted, remove them from the oven. Drizzle with the balsamic glaze and toss gently to coat.
- Garnish with sea salt flakes and freshly ground black pepper to taste.
- Serve immediately as a side dish for any meal.

Nutrition per serving (approximate):

- Calories: 200-250
- Fat: 10-15g
- Carbohydrates: 30-35g
- Fiber: 5-7g
- Protein: 5-7g
- Sodium: 200-300mg (depending on salt and balsamic vinegar)

Tips:

- Feel free to substitute or add other vegetables like mushrooms, Brussels sprouts, or carrots.
- For a vegan option, omit the honey or maple syrup and use agave nectar instead.

Creamy Mashed Potatoes with Garlic and Herbs:

Ingredients (serves 4-6):

- 4 large russet potatoes, peeled and cut into 1-inch cubes
- 1/2 cup (1 stick) unsalted butter, softened
- 1/2 cup sour cream or plain Greek yogurt
- 1/4 cup heavy cream (optional, for extra creaminess)
- 2 cloves garlic, minced
- 1/2 teaspoon dried thyme
- 1/4 teaspoon dried parsley
- Salt and freshly ground black pepper, to taste
- Chopped fresh herbs (optional, such as chives, parsley, or dill) for garnish

Instructions:
- Place the cubed potatoes in a large pot and cover with cold water. Add 1 teaspoon of salt and bring to a boil over high heat. Reduce heat to medium and simmer for 15-20 minutes, or until the potatoes are fork-tender.
- Drain the potatoes and return them to the pot. Using a potato masher or hand mixer, mash the potatoes until smooth.
- Add the butter, sour cream or yogurt, heavy cream (if using), garlic, thyme, parsley, salt, and pepper to the mashed potatoes. Beat until well combined and creamy.
- Taste and adjust seasonings as needed. If the mashed potatoes are too thick, add a splash of milk or water until you reach your desired consistency.
- Serve immediately, garnished with fresh chopped herbs (optional).

Nutrition per serving (approximate):
- Calories: 350-400
- Fat: 20-25g
- Carbohydrates: 45-50g
- Fiber: 2-3g
- Protein: 5-7g
- Sodium: 300-400mg (depending on added salt and ingredients)

Tips:
- For an extra rich flavor, roast the garlic cloves before mincing them.
- You can use Yukon Gold potatoes instead of russet potatoes for a slightly creamier texture.
- Leftover mashed potatoes can be stored in an airtight container in the refrigerator for up to 3 days. Reheat gently in a saucepan with a splash of milk or water

Green Bean Casserole with Crispy Onions:
This classic holiday dish can be enjoyed by everyone, even with different dietary needs and preferences. Choose the option that best suits you:

Option 1: Traditional Creamy Green Bean Casserole
Ingredients (serves 4-6):
- 1 pound fresh green beans, trimmed and snapped
- 1 tablespoon olive oil
- 1/2 cup chopped onion
- 2 cloves garlic, minced

- 1 (10 3/4-ounce) can condensed cream of mushroom soup
- 1 cup milk
- 1/2 teaspoon salt
- 1/4 teaspoon black pepper
- 1/2 cup French fried onions, divided

Instructions:
- Preheat the oven to 350°F (175°C).
- Bring a large pot of salted water to a boil. Add green beans and cook for 5 minutes, or until tender-crisp. Drain and set aside.
- In a large skillet, heat olive oil over medium heat. Add onion and cook until softened, about 5 minutes. Stir in garlic and cook for 30 seconds, until fragrant.
- In a bowl, whisk together cream of mushroom soup, milk, salt, and pepper. Add the onion and garlic to the skillet and bring to a simmer.
- Stir in cooked green beans and half of the crispy onions. Pour the mixture into a greased 9x13 inch baking dish.
- Top with the remaining crispy onions and bake for 15-20 minutes, or until bubbly and golden brown.

Nutrition per serving (approximate):
- Calories: 350-400
- Fat: 15-20g
- Carbohydrates: 40-45g
- Fiber: 3-4g
- Protein: 15-20g
- Sodium: 600-700mg (depending on soup)

Option 2: Lighter Green Bean Casserole with Almond Milk

Ingredients (serves 4-6):
- 1 pound fresh green beans, trimmed and snapped
- 1 tablespoon olive oil
- 1/2 cup chopped onion
- 2 cloves garlic, minced
- 1 (10 3/4-ounce) can low-fat cream of mushroom soup
- 1 cup unsweetened almond milk
- 1/2 teaspoon salt
- 1/4 teaspoon black pepper
- 1/2 cup chopped walnuts or pecans, toasted
- 1/4 cup reduced-fat cheddar cheese, grated (optional)

Instructions:
- Follow steps 1-3 from Option 1.
- In a bowl, whisk together cream of mushroom soup, almond milk, salt, and pepper. Add the onion and garlic to the skillet and bring to a simmer.
- Stir in cooked green beans and walnuts or pecans. Pour the mixture into a greased 9x13 inch baking dish.
- Top with cheddar cheese (if using) and bake for 15-20 minutes, or until bubbly and golden brown.

Nutrition per serving (approximate):
- Calories: 250-300
- Fat: 10-15g
- Carbohydrates: 35-40g
- Fiber: 4-5g
- Protein: 10-15g
- Sodium: 400-500mg (depending on soup)

Tips:

- For a vegan option, use vegan cream of mushroom soup and vegan butter for the roux.
- You can substitute breadcrumbs for the crispy onions for a gluten-free option.
- Add other vegetables like mushrooms, carrots, or peas for more flavor and nutrients.
- Adjust the seasonings to your taste.

Cranberry Orange Sauce: A Tart & Tangy Holiday Staple

Ingredients:

- 12 ounces fresh cranberries
- 1 cup freshly squeezed orange juice (from about 2-3 oranges)
- 1/2 cup granulated sugar
- 1/4 cup water
- 1 orange, zested and thinly sliced (optional)
- 1 cinnamon stick
- 1/4 teaspoon ground ginger
- Pinch of salt

Instructions:

- In a large saucepan, combine cranberries, orange juice, sugar, water, orange zest (if using), cinnamon stick, ginger, and salt.
- Bring to a boil over medium heat, then reduce heat to low and simmer for 15-20 minutes, stirring occasionally, until cranberries have softened and sauce thickens slightly.
- If using sliced oranges, add them to the pot during the last 5 minutes of simmering for additional flavor and texture.
- Remove from heat and discard cinnamon stick.
- Let the sauce cool slightly before serving.

Nutrition per serving (approximate):

- Calories: 60-70
- Fat: 0g
- Carbohydrates: 15-16g
- Fiber: 1g
- Sugar: 12-13g
- Protein: 0g
- Vitamin C: 20% Daily Value

Tips:

- For a smoother sauce, use an immersion blender after simmering to purée some of the cranberries.
- This sauce can be made ahead of time and stored in the refrigerator for up to 5 days. Reheat gently before serving.
- The sauce can also be frozen for up to 3 months. Thaw overnight in the refrigerator before using.
- Feel free to adjust the sweetness to your liking. You can use less sugar or add a splash of honey or maple syrup for a slightly different flavor.

Stuffed Portobello Mushrooms with Quinoa and Feta:

Ingredients (serves 4-6):

For the mushrooms:
- 4 large portobello mushrooms (stems removed and cleaned)
- 1 tablespoon olive oil
- Salt and pepper to taste

For the quinoa filling:
- 1 cup quinoa, rinsed
- 1 1/2 cups vegetable broth
- 1/2 cup chopped onion
- 2 cloves garlic, minced
- 1/2 cup chopped bell pepper (any color)
- 1/4 cup chopped sun-dried tomatoes (not oil-packed)
- 1/4 cup chopped fresh parsley
- 1/2 cup crumbled feta cheese
- 1/4 teaspoon dried thyme
- Salt and pepper to taste

Instructions:
- Preheat the oven to 400°F (200°C).
- Prepare the mushrooms: Drizzle the portobello mushrooms with olive oil and season with salt and pepper. Place them on a baking sheet, gill side up, and roast for 10-12 minutes.
- Cook the quinoa: In a medium saucepan, combine quinoa and vegetable broth. Bring to a boil, then reduce heat and simmer for 15 minutes, or until quinoa is cooked and fluffy. Fluff with a fork and set aside.
- Sauté the vegetables: While the quinoa is cooking, heat olive oil in a large skillet over medium heat. Add onion and garlic, and cook until softened, about 5 minutes.
- Stir in bell pepper and sun-dried tomatoes, and cook for another 2-3 minutes until softened.
- Assemble the filling: In a large bowl, combine cooked quinoa, sautéed vegetables, parsley, feta cheese, thyme, salt, and pepper. Mix well to combine.
- Stuff the mushrooms: Spoon the quinoa mixture into the pre-roasted portobello mushrooms, filling them evenly.
- Bake and serve: Return the stuffed mushrooms to the oven and bake for 10-15 minutes, or until heated through and slightly golden brown on top.
- Serve immediately while hot, garnished with additional parsley or a drizzle of balsamic glaze (optional).

Nutrition per serving (approximate):
- Calories: 350-400
- Fat: 10-15g
- Carbohydrates: 45-50g
- Fiber: 5-7g
- Protein: 15-20g
- Sodium: 300-400mg (depending on broth and feta cheese)

Tips:

- For a richer flavor, add a splash of balsamic vinegar to the pan after adding the garlic.
- You can use any type of bell pepper you like, or a combination of different colors.

- If you don't have sun-dried tomatoes, you can substitute with chopped fresh tomatoes or 1/4 cup of tomato paste.
- Add a pinch of red pepper flakes or a chopped chili pepper for a touch of heat.

Lentil Soup with Crusty Bread:

Ingredients (serves 4-6):
- 1 tablespoon olive oil
- 1 onion, chopped
- 2 carrots, chopped
- 2 celery stalks, chopped
- 2 cloves garlic, minced
- 1 cup green lentils, rinsed
- 4 cups vegetable broth
- 1 (28-ounce) can crushed tomatoes
- 1 teaspoon dried thyme
- 1/2 teaspoon dried oregano
- Salt and freshly ground black pepper, to taste
- Optional toppings: Chopped fresh parsley, lemon wedges, hot sauce, crusty bread

Instructions:
- Heat olive oil in a large pot or Dutch oven over medium heat. Add onion, carrots, and celery, and cook until softened, about 5 minutes.
- Add garlic and cook for 30 seconds until fragrant.
- Stir in lentils, vegetable broth, crushed tomatoes, thyme, and oregano. Season with salt and pepper to taste.

- Bring to a boil, then reduce heat to low and simmer for 30-40 minutes, or until lentils are tender and the soup has thickened. Be sure to stir occasionally and adjust seasonings as needed.
- Serve hot with your desired toppings. Enjoy!

Nutrition per serving (approximate):
- Calories: 300-350
- Fat: 10-15g
- Carbohydrates: 40-45g
- Fiber: 8-10g
- Protein: 20-25g
- Sodium: 500-600mg (depending on broth and tomato sauce)

Tips:
- For a richer flavor, add a splash of red wine to the pan after adding the garlic.
- You can use pre-cooked lentils to save time, but be sure to adjust the cooking time accordingly.
- Add a pinch of red pepper flakes or a chopped chili pepper for a touch of heat.

Roasted Sweet Potato Salad with Pecans and Cranberries:

Ingredients (serves 4-6):
- 2 large sweet potatoes, peeled and cubed
- 1 tablespoon olive oil
- 1/2 teaspoon salt
- 1/4 teaspoon black pepper
- 1/2 cup pecan halves, toasted
- 1/2 cup dried cranberries
- 1/4 cup chopped red onion
- 2 tablespoons fresh parsley, chopped (optional)

For the dressing:
- 2 tablespoons olive oil
- 1 tablespoon Dijon mustard
- 1 tablespoon apple cider vinegar
- 1 teaspoon honey
- 1/4 teaspoon salt
- 1/4 teaspoon black pepper

Instructions:
- Preheat the oven to 400°F (200°C). Line a baking sheet with parchment paper.
- Toss sweet potato cubes with olive oil, salt, and pepper. Spread evenly on the prepared baking sheet.
- Roast for 20-25 minutes, or until tender and lightly browned.
- While the sweet potatoes roast, toast the pecans in a dry skillet over medium heat until fragrant, about 5 minutes. Set aside to cool.
- In a small bowl, whisk together the dressing ingredients until smooth.
- Once the sweet potatoes are cooked, transfer them to a large bowl. Let cool slightly.
- Add the toasted pecans, dried cranberries, red onion, and parsley (if using) to the sweet potatoes.
- Pour the dressing over the salad and toss gently to combine.
- Serve warm or at room temperature.

Nutrition per serving (approximate):
- Calories: 350-400
- Fat: 15-20g
- Carbohydrates: 45-50g
- Fiber: 5-6g
- Protein: 5-6g
- Sodium: 300-400mg (depending on salt intake)

Tips:
- For a smoky flavor, add a pinch of smoked paprika to the dressing.
- You can substitute walnuts or almonds for the pecans

Spiced Apple Cider:
Ingredients (makes 4-6 servings):
- 4 cups apple cider (unsweetened and unfiltered preferred)
- 1 orange, sliced
- 1 lemon, sliced
- 2 cinnamon sticks
- 4 whole cloves
- 1/2 teaspoon grated nutmeg (or 1/4 teaspoon ground)
- 1/4 teaspoon ground ginger (optional)
- Honey or maple syrup (optional, to taste)

Instructions:

- Combine all ingredients in a large pot or slow cooker.
- If using a pot, bring to a simmer over medium heat. If using a slow cooker, cook on low for 2-3 hours, or on high for 1-2 hours.
- Let the cider simmer for 15-20 minutes, allowing the flavors to infuse.
- Strain the cider through a fine-mesh sieve to remove the fruit slices and spices.
- Return the cider to the pot or slow cooker, and heat through.
- Taste and adjust sweetness with honey or maple syrup, if desired.
- Serve warm in mugs, garnished with a cinnamon stick slice and an orange or lemon wedge, if desired.

Nutrition per serving (approximate):

- Calories: 100-120
- Fat: 0g
- Carbohydrates: 25-30g
- Fiber: 2-3g
- Sugar: 15-20g
- Protein: 0g
- Sodium: 10-15mg

Tips:

- For a richer flavor, add a splash of apple brandy or bourbon before serving.
- You can also substitute pear or cranberry juice for some of the apple cider.
- Add a few cranberries to the pot for a festive touch.

Vegan Eggnog with Cashew Milk and Spices:

Ingredients (makes 4-6 servings):

- 1 cup raw cashews, soaked for at least 4 hours or overnight
- 4 cups unsweetened cashew milk
- 1/2 cup pitted Medjool dates
- 1 teaspoon vanilla extract
- 1/2 teaspoon ground cinnamon
- 1/4 teaspoon ground nutmeg
- 1/8 teaspoon ground cardamom (optional)
- Pinch of sea salt
- Freshly grated nutmeg, for garnish (optional)

- Drain the soaked cashews and rinse well.
- Combine the cashews, cashew milk, dates, vanilla extract, cinnamon, nutmeg, cardamom (if using), and salt in a high-powered blender. Blend until smooth and creamy, about 2 minutes.
- If the mixture is too thick, add more cashew milk, 1 tablespoon at a time, until desired consistency is reached.
- Chill the eggnog in the refrigerator for at least 2 hours, or overnight for a richer flavor.

Instructions:

- Serve chilled in glasses, garnished with freshly grated nutmeg (optional).

Nutrition per serving (approximate):
- Calories: 250-300
- Fat: 15-20g
- Carbohydrates: 25-30g
- Fiber: 3-4g
- Protein: 4-5g
- Sugar: 10-15g
- Sodium: 150-200mg

Tips:
- For a thicker eggnog, use less cashew milk or add 1 tablespoon of chia seeds and blend after adding all the other ingredients. Let the mixture sit for 10 minutes to thicken before chilling.
- You can adjust the sweetness to your preference by adding or reducing the number of dates.
- This eggnog will keep in the refrigerator for up to 4 days.

Rosemary Garlic Roasted Chicken:

Ingredients (serves 4-6):
- 1 whole chicken (4-5 lbs)
- 2 tablespoons olive oil
- 2 tablespoons chopped fresh rosemary, or 1 tablespoon dried rosemary
- 4 cloves garlic, minced
- 1 teaspoon salt
- 1/2 teaspoon black pepper
- Optional: Lemon wedges, for serving

Instructions:
- Preheat the oven to 425°F (220°C).
- Pat the chicken dry with paper towels, and remove any giblets from the cavity.
- In a small bowl, combine olive oil, rosemary, garlic, salt, and pepper.
- Rub the mixture all over the chicken, under the skin, and inside the cavity.
- Place the chicken breast-side up on a roasting rack set over a baking dish.
- Tie the legs together with kitchen twine for even cooking (optional).
- Roast for 1 hour, or until the internal temperature of the thickest part of the thigh reaches 165°F (74°C).
- Baste the chicken with pan juices halfway through roasting for extra flavor (optional).
- Let the chicken rest for 10-15 minutes before carving and serving.

Nutrition per serving (approximate):
- Calories: 500-600
- Fat: 30-40g
- Carbohydrates: 2-3g
- Protein: 50-60g
- Sodium: 500-600mg (depending on salt and broth)

Tips:
- For even crispier skin, pat the chicken dry before seasoning.
- Stuff the cavity with lemon wedges or fresh herbs for an additional layer of flavor.
- Add chopped root vegetables like potatoes, carrots, and onions to the

bottom of the pan for a complete meal.

- Drizzle the pan juices over the carved chicken for extra moisture and flavor.

Baked Brie with Cranberry and Pecan Compote:

Ingredients:

For the compote:

- 1 cup fresh cranberries
- 1/4 cup brown sugar
- 1/4 cup water
- 1/4 teaspoon ground cinnamon
- 1/4 teaspoon ground nutmeg
- 1 tablespoon orange juice
- 1 tablespoon chopped walnuts

For the brie:

- 1 (8-ounce) round brie cheese, rind removed
- 1/4 cup chopped pecans
- 1 tablespoon honey
- Fresh rosemary sprigs (optional), for garnish

Instructions:

Make the compote:

- In a small saucepan, combine cranberries, brown sugar, water, cinnamon, nutmeg, and orange juice. Bring to a simmer over medium heat.
- Cook for 10-15 minutes, stirring occasionally, until cranberries soften and sauce thickens slightly.
- Remove from heat and stir in chopped walnuts.

Prepare the brie:

- Preheat the oven to 375°F (190°C).
- Place the brie cheese on a baking sheet lined with parchment paper.
- Score the top of the brie in a diamond pattern with a sharp knife.
- Scatter chopped pecans over the top of the brie.
- Drizzle with honey.

Bake the brie:

- Bake for 15-20 minutes, or until the cheese is softened and bubbly.
- Remove from oven and let cool for 5 minutes before serving.

Serve:

- Spoon the cranberry compote around the brie.
- Garnish with fresh rosemary sprigs (optional), and serve with crackers or baguette slices.

Nutrition per serving (approximate):

- Calories: 450-500
- Fat: 25-30g
- Carbohydrates: 40-45g
- Fiber: 3-4g
- Protein: 15-20g
- Sodium: 300-400mg (depending on cheese and honey)

Tips:

- You can use other nuts instead of walnuts, such as almonds or pistachios.
- For a sweeter compote, add a little extra honey or maple syrup.
- If you don't have fresh rosemary, you can use other herbs like thyme or sage.

- This recipe can be easily doubled or tripled for a larger group.

Dark Chocolate Bark with Dried Fruits and Nuts:

Ingredients (makes approximately 12 servings):
- 8 ounces dark chocolate chips (60% or higher cacao content)
- 1 tablespoon coconut oil (optional)
- 1/2 cup dried cranberries
- 1/2 cup dried cherries
- 1/4 cup chopped almonds
- 1/4 cup chopped pistachios
- Pinch of sea salt (optional)

Instructions:
- Line a baking sheet with parchment paper.
- In a medium bowl, melt the dark chocolate chips and coconut oil (if using) in a microwave at 30-second intervals, stirring until smooth. Be careful not to overheat.
- Pour the melted chocolate onto the prepared baking sheet and spread into an even layer using a spatula.
- Sprinkle the dried fruit and nuts evenly over the chocolate.
- Refrigerate for at least 2 hours, or until the chocolate is set.
- Once set, break the bark into pieces and enjoy!

Nutrition per serving (approximate):
- Calories: 150-170
- Fat: 10-12g
- Carbohydrates: 15-18g
- Fiber: 2-3g
- Protein: 2-3g
- Sodium: 30-40mg

Tips:
- You can adjust the type and amount of dried fruit and nuts to your preference. Some other good options include chopped apricots, mango, walnuts, or pecans.
- For a more festive touch, add a sprinkle of sea salt, edible glitter, or crushed peppermint candies before refrigerating.
- Store the bark in an airtight container in the refrigerator for up to 2 weeks.

Peppermint Fudge with Almond Milk: A Dairy-Free Holiday Treat

Ingredients (makes approximately 20 squares):
- 1/2 cup vegan butter (or dairy-free butter alternative)
- 1 cup unsweetened cocoa powder
- 1/2 cup vegan powdered sugar (or monk fruit sweetener)
- 1/4 cup almond milk
- 1/4 cup pure maple syrup
- 1/2 teaspoon vanilla extract
- 1/4 teaspoon peppermint extract
- Pinch of salt (optional)
- Crushed candy canes or peppermint sprinkles (optional, for topping)

Instructions:
- Line an 8x8 inch baking dish with parchment paper.

- In a medium saucepan over medium heat, melt the vegan butter. Whisk in the cocoa powder until smooth and no lumps remain.
- Stir in the almond milk, maple syrup, vanilla extract, peppermint extract, and salt (if using). Bring to a simmer, stirring constantly, and cook for 2-3 minutes until slightly thickened.
- Remove from heat and pour the fudge mixture into the prepared baking dish. Smooth the top evenly with a spatula.
- Refrigerate for at least 2 hours, or until the fudge is set and firm.
- Once set, lift the fudge out of the pan using the parchment paper overhang. Cut into squares and top with crushed candy canes, or peppermint sprinkles, if desired.
- Store leftover fudge in an airtight container in the refrigerator for up to one week.

Nutrition per serving (approximate):
- Calories: 150-170
- Fat: 10-12g
- Carbohydrates: 18-20g
- Fiber: 1-2g
- Protein: 1-2g
- Sodium: 50-60mg

Tips:
- For a richer chocolate flavor, use dark cocoa powder.
- You can substitute almond milk with other dairy-free alternatives like oat milk or coconut milk.
- Adjust the amount of maple syrup to your desired sweetness level.
- Get creative with toppings! Try chopped nuts, dried cranberries, or even a drizzle of vegan chocolate sauce.

Printed in Great Britain
by Amazon

44815705R00090